Carol Bacchi was born in Montreal, Canada, and migrated to Australia in 1976. She and her son Stephen, live in Adelaide where she teaches in the Politics Department, University of Adelaide. Her other books include *The Politics of Affirmative Action* (Sage, 1996) and *Women, Policy and Politics: The Construction of Policy Problems* (1999).

FEAR OF FOOD:

A Diary of Mothering

Carol Lee Bacchi

Spinifex Press Pty Ltd
504 Queensberry Street
North Melbourne, Vic. 3051
Australia

women@spinifexpresss.com.au
http://www.spinifexpress.com.au

First published 2003
Copyright © Carol Lee Bacchi

Cover design by Deb Snibson
Typeset in Stone Informal by Palmer Higgs Pty Ltd
Printed and bound by McPhersons Printing Group

National Library of Australia
Cataloguing-in-Publication data:
Bacchi, Carol Lee, 1948–.
    Fear of Food: A Diary of Mothering.

ISBN 1 876756 32 2.

    1. Children - Nutrition. 2. Eating disorders. 3. Children
    - Nutrition - Psychological aspects. I. Title.

618.9239

To Stephen

Acknowledgements

The people who helped me through this difficult time are mentioned in the text but I have changed most of their names to guarantee their privacy. My brother, Don, and his wife, Rhonda, deserve to be singled out. Their willingness to disrupt their tranquility by taking my son and me into their home for six weeks will always be remembered with gratitude. I also want to acknowledge the help of my dear friends in Canberra and in Sydney who stood by us even when this must not have been easy to do.

My sincere thanks to Greg de Cure, Chris Beasley, Zoe Gill, Robert Dare, Christine Finnimore, Lisa Hill, Fred Guilhaus, Anne Yeomans and Paul Corcoran for their thoughtful comments and suggestions. I am also grateful to the readers at Spinifex for drawing to my attention important lacunae in the narrative, and to my editor, Barbara Burton, for her attention to detail. And, of course, I need to thank my son for giving me a reason to endure and for strengthening my conviction that telling our story is a worthwhile thing to do.

Preface

This is a story about my first and only experience of mothering, and of the ways in which my infant son's feeding disorder affected that experience. It is difficult to put dates to the problem. Medically, it probably began when he contracted viral pharangytis, a severe throat infection, at three months and ended some time in his sixth month. But my view is that the problem had earlier origins and lasted much longer. I believe that our difficulties around feeding had their beginnings in my early attempts at breastfeeding, attempts that failed due to my lack of milk. And I believe that our difficulties have only recently been resolved (at the time of writing the book, late 2001, my son was eight years old). Perhaps this is why I am now able to write about them.

My account differs from the medical account primarily because I include myself as a part of the problem. I do not mean that I blame myself. Let me make that very clear. I am opposed to all forms of mother-bashing, laying guilt trips on mothers. When I say that I include myself as part of the problem I mean that in *my* head the problem started earlier and lasted longer. Because of this, I had difficulties with feeding my son that go beyond any kind of medical diagnosis.

It is also unclear, as you will see, whether all doctors or nurses would agree that my son had a feeding disorder for the three months he was treated. For many of them, to say that he had a feeding disorder meant that he suffered some form of physiological difficulty, a sore throat or reflux. For many of them, the fact that he rejected food was not sufficient to constitute a feeding disorder. For these medical people, the problem was that I was a 'tense' mother or that I had post-natal depression or that I didn't enjoy my child.

I believe that it is possible to say that part of the problem was in my head without psychologising the problem in the way these explanations tend to. Stephen rejected food because of the dynamic established between us which was due to a number of physiological conditions including failed breast-feeding, colic/reflux, viral pharangytis, congestion due to colds, teething, and so on. This account is an attempt to examine the nature of that dynamic.

I wrote Diaries for the first nine months of my son's life. I also had separate Feeding/Sleeping Records which kept track of when he fed, how much he consumed (once he was on the bottle), when he slept and details about other bodily functions such as bowel movements. It came as quite a shock to me to discover that I remembered things quite differently from the story these records tell. The dates seemed wrong. And some of the incidents seemed out of order. I don't remember them in this order.

Which account should I offer you? The account in the Diaries and Feeding/Sleeping Records should be closer to the truth, shouldn't it? After all, they were written at the time. But, as you will find out, I was in a state of near exhaustion during much of the period they describe. I don't think I was really 'all there' much of the time. It is completely possible then that events as related in the Diaries are filtered and distorted.

Moreover, how I remember this period deserves attention. It is my memories, after all, which I live with and which continue at some level to puzzle me. It is my memories that impel me to revisit the nightmare, to try to make some sense of it. But, as I've mentioned, my memories often don't match the Diaries. Are my memories illusory? Or, does the fact that they are my memories make them 'true' in some sense or other?

I have decided to combine the accounts, to offer current reflections interspersed with excerpts from the narrative Diaries and from the Feeding/Sleeping Records. Passages from the latter sources appear in italics to suggest the haze within which they were produced; current reflections appear in normal type.

I have memories of testing times. I nearly said 'terrible times', but I felt that I needed to soften that. I changed 'terrible' to 'testing' because I didn't want you to conclude that nothing good happened during these months. I didn't want you to think that my experience of early motherhood was *all* bad. I mean, it is serious enough that I should suggest that the experience wasn't *totally* wonderful. The conventional picture of motherhood as some natural state of joy and bonding makes it difficult, if not impossible, to admit how very gruelling mothering can be.

I believe that there are mothers out there—fathers too—who will recognise themselves in this account. I do not regard my experiences as unique. Rather they are somewhere on a continuum of the challenges accompanying mothering. My hope is that my willingness to disclose my 'testing times' will make it easier for other mothers to give voice to the mix of experiences which is motherhood, the euphoria as well as the frustration, the warm glow as well as the quiet desperation.

Beyond this, I hope that the personal catharsis achieved in the telling of our story sheds some light on the complex dynamic between mother and child, medical professionals, and the wider society. Throughout, I highlight the conditions—institutional inflexibility, social isolation (doubtless compounded by my single parent status), medical orthodoxy—which exacerbated the difficulties my son and I faced. Things needn't have been so bleak. These months were the closest to hell that I've ever come. But then I've led a sheltered life. My hell won't measure high on the Richter scale of hells. But it may just register a reading.

The conditions under which I became pregnant are not relevant to the story, except to say that I never set out to raise a child on my own. It just worked out that way. I wrote the narrative Diaries and kept the Feeding Records for a complex mix of reasons which are discussed in the text. Primarily, they served the purpose of keeping me company and keeping me sane. I never intended them to become part of a public record.

I decided our story was worth telling due largely to the personal confidences of other mothers about the difficulties they faced during mothering. Through these shared intimacies I came to realise that there is a side to mothering which is seldom discussed—the daily challenges, the social isolation, the uncertainty and trepidation accompanying almost sole responsibility for one, or more than one, small vulnerable human being. My particular experiences fell into context as one version of a common tale— the story of real, gritty, down-to-earth mothering. The goal in relating these experiences is to prick the balloon of idealised mothering which makes it so difficult to admit, to oneself and to others, that mothering can be frightening, exhausting and, even at times, downright demoralising.

I approached motherhood much as I would any new experience. To me, it was a wonderful, exciting adventure—which indeed it is! I was euphoric the day I found out I was pregnant. In the months leading up to the birth, I would walk on Black Mountain or swim in a nearby Olympic pool, talking in my head to my son-to-be about the wonderful things we would do together. I knew that I was expecting a son because, on medical advice, I had undergone chorionic villus sampling—a procedure for detecting birth 'defects' in the first trimester.

When, after Stephen's birth, things became difficult, I encountered a barrage of advice from institutional experts who told me what I was doing 'wrong'. There was little interest in me except to the extent that I was or was not following the often contradictory rules they endorsed—for feeding, for sleeps, for caring. I was judged against these standards and was repeatedly found wanting. These sorts of interventions did not help Stephen and me; they made the experience worse. This story then is a plea to refocus on mothers as more than reproducers of the next generation, to see them as flesh and blood human beings doing their best to cope with a range of often daunting daily challenges. This refocusing, I suggest, is a necessary first step to identifying the kinds of institutional changes which could improve the reality of mothering.

Chapter 1

Hell

'He won't eat,' I stated simply.

'He's just stubborn,' the nurse replied.

'He won't eat,' I insisted a little more strongly. I was feeling fragile.

'We have our ways of making him eat,' she said. I swear I could see a smirk on her face, almost as if she were enjoying this. The question was—did she enjoy the idea of making my six-month old son eat? Or did she enjoy the prospect of proving me wrong and, incidentally, of proving herself right? I felt that I had been injected into a B grade film. I mean really—'we have our ways of making him eat'.

And so, here I found myself at one of the many specialist hospitals set up to help mothers who are not coping (hereafter referred to as Mothers' Hospitals). The women are not coping for any number of reasons, it seems. I almost envied the women who were there because their nipples were painful and cracked, and who needed assistance with breastfeeding. At least, they had a *physical* problem. You could feel sorry for them. But my problem (perhaps I should say our, my son's and my problem, but it felt like my problem and everyone seemed to want me to believe that it was *my* problem) was in my head, in my disposition, in my failed mothering. I was called a 'tense mother', not for the first time. A tense mother—what did this mean? It sounded like I was an uptight mother, a frantic mother, an out-of-control mother. Some of this felt right, but not really. Things just hadn't turned out as I had expected them to. And no one could explain why.

The first time I wrote the above paragraph, I had written 'stressed mother'. I knew the word 'stressed' wasn't quite right but I couldn't at the moment remember the word 'tense'. I knew that 'stressed' wasn't right because in the current vernacular being stressed is quite respectable, or at the very least it is expected. Everyone is stressed. There is even a café nearby called 'Stressed Out'. The term 'stressed' suggests that something is doing the stressing *to* you. The word 'tense' by contrast implies something *in* you. They even describe it as a syndrome—the tense mother syndrome. This meant that I had a condition or perhaps more accurately that I *was* a condition. After all, I *was* the tense mother.

This trip to the Mothers' Hospital (17 May 1993) is the middle of the nightmare. It is probably the worst part. I will never forget sitting in a far-off corner of the nursery watching that diabolical woman forcing my child to eat. Since I said he wouldn't take food from me, her task was to show me that he would

3

take food from her, that he was 'just stubborn'. She shoved the bottle in his mouth. He tried to push it away. He was screaming. She shoved spoonfuls of pap in his mouth. He wouldn't open his mouth, except to scream. And then she shoved the spoon in. He spluttered. He choked. I cried quietly.

So, how had we come to this? Stephen was born in early December 1992. He breastfed, unhappily, for six weeks. He had 'colic' from infancy which developed into 'reflux' by age two months (February 1993). Feeding him, getting him to take a bottle, was not easy. In mid-March he was hospitalised with viral pharangytis. Increasingly, Stephen rejected food, pushing away bottles and screaming. His poor feeds meant short and unpredictable sleeps. Worn down, I turned to the Mothers' Hospital in early April and again in middle April 1993. We returned for a day clinic on 17 May. This is the day of the 'forced feeding' episode described above. On 21 May we were admitted for four nights. On this occasion, hospital staff sedated Stephen to feed and in the end sent us home with no resolution to the problem. It took several months with the support of friends to emerge from the nightmare. This is our story.

Chapter 2

At the Breast

I was an elderly primigravida (older first time mother). Or rather I was *called* an elderly primigravida. The distinction is important. The first description implies that this is how I saw myself; the second leaves my self-perception undetermined.

You may have gathered that I object to having myself put into categories. I may as well confess that I am an academic and that I have written a good deal about feminist theory. I hope that doesn't put you off. This is not an academic book. It is the personal account of a mother who happens to work in a university.

Part of this account will be about the meeting of feminism and motherhood, a sensitive and dangerous topic. In some accounts, feminists are supposed to be dedicated to saving women *from* maternity. This sits uncomfortably, of course, with the large numbers of feminists who *are* mothers. I can almost hear people thinking that my feminism may somehow explain all the problems I had. Indeed, maybe it does explain some of them. But I assure you that no single factor could explain *all* of them. That, in fact, is what I want to write about. I want to avoid simple explanations. Syndromes and categories, it seems to me, are simple explanations; hence, my discomfort with them.

I was forty-four years old when I became pregnant with Stephen. This, as mentioned, put me into the category of elderly primigravida, which means simply that I was a little older than most women when they have their first child. But the repercussions are by no means simple. Being of a certain age for your first child means that you are automatically considered a high-risk pregnancy. This is so, regardless of how fit you are, and I was extremely fit when I became pregnant. In my head, I tried to deny the implications of being labelled 'high risk', but we shouldn't ignore the impact of medical diagnoses on our psyche. In fact, you could say that being called 'high risk' was not a way to make you feel relaxed about your pregnancy. Dare I say, it may even have encouraged a first-time mother to feel just a little tense.

In the event, the pregnancy went well and so did the birth. There was a small glitch when Stephen's heart was faltering and the specialist was rushed in (around 5 a.m.) but this sorted itself out almost immediately once he arrived. In fact, I can recall him making a little joke about how the heart picked up the moment another male entered the room— suggesting an early episode of male bonding. The specialist knew about my feminism, of course. I put his attempted jest down to this.

My first problems began after the birth, and they seemed consistently to be around feeding. My colostrum[1] came in late, which was not exceptional I was told, but this meant that little Stephen had to work very hard for any food and that he screamed almost continually. Now, many people will tell you how difficult it is to stay calm while your child is crying in great distress. But they don't tell you about the knot in your stomach, the one that tightens with each wail. I walked the hospital corridors for hours each day and night trying to get Stephen to sleep. I can recall one nurse saying, 'There always seems to be one who gets to walk the corridors.' I was just wondering why it had to be me.

Stephen was born in late 1992. At this time the Breast is Better Brigade were dominant, at least in the hospital I was in. One evening, in desperation, a kindly nurse who could see how tired I was arranged for a formula top-up. She explained that some doctors and nurses feared that this could turn a baby off the breast, but she didn't accept this. I had a decent sleep for the first time that night.

They sent me home after five days. I didn't really want to go home. Stephen still wasn't feeding well

---

1   This is the thin milky secretion which precedes true lactation.

and as a result he slept little and screamed a great deal. On my last day, an older nurse spoke to me. She said that she didn't want to be negative but that my age might mean that I wouldn't produce enough milk, that I might not be able to breastfeed. It's funny, you know, but I wouldn't have minded this at all. I can tell you that it was far from a warm bonding experience—the all-too-conventional image of breastfeeding— to have poor little Stephen sucking for up to an hour on each breast, with only two hourly breaks. The problem was that it was implied that somehow if I couldn't breastfeed, I was letting Stephen down. I wasn't giving him the start in life he deserved. God knows what would follow— low IQ? hyperactivity? vandalism?

I now recall fondly my French Canadian friend's encounter with the Breast is Better Brigade. Her name is Yvonne and she speaks broken English with a most charming accent. When she was offered her third child to breastfeed, she put a halt to the proceedings in no uncertain terms. 'I told dem,' she reported, 'I told dem dat I did not want to breastfeed. I told dem dat my breasts, my breasts were for my husband. Dey left me alone after dat.'

But I wanted to be a 'good mother' and so I persisted. This meant that in those first days at home I never managed more than two hours sleep at a time, an all-too-common experience for new mothers. You must recall that my body was battered to begin with. I once heard that giving birth is the equivalent to running three marathons. This sounds impressive but the analogy is too pretty for my liking. It implies a lot of sweat and some sore muscles. And it conjures up the image of the super athlete, an icon of our times. I had piles and I was still bleeding. I don't think I quite measured up for icon status.

I have records of Stephen's feeds from our arrival home until he reached 9 months old. I call these the Feeding Records. For the early period these indicate when he fed and how long he fed on each breast. They also keep track of bowel motions, recorded as b/o (bowel opened). The later records, post-breastfeeding, record the time of each feed and the amount consumed. They include 'b/o's' and, later, doses of medication. Finally, in the last few months they include a summary of Stephen's sleeps, the length of each and how often he needed to be 'resettled'. I also kept narrative Diaries. At the beginning these were daily unless something intervened, like being rushed into emergency with Stephen in the middle of the night. The entries become fewer in number towards the end and then stop.

When I reread my collected diaries and records in preparation to write this memoir, I was surprised and indeed distressed to find that there were Feeding Records for the breastfeeding days. I thought that I had kept records only when it became possible to measure the amounts Stephen had consumed, to see if he was drinking enough. These pre-bottle Feeding Records seemed to signal an early obsession with feeding Stephen. But then I remembered that I had been instructed by nursing staff to keep track of which breast he 'ended' on, so that I would 'start' him on the other one at the next feed—a practice recommended to ensure 'equal time' and hence adequate flow.

The first Feeding Record appears for 12 December, 1992. Stephen was ten days old and we had been home from hospital for five days. The record is a scrawl. I reproduce it here.

1. *2 a.m.*
2. *6.15–8 a.m. (slept 8–9 a.m., 1 hour)*
3. *9.30*
4. *1.00–2.20*
5. *4.15 (settled 5.50 pm; [corrected to] 6.20 p.m.)*
6. *9.55 p.m. (settled 11.20 p.m.; arrow to 4 a.m.* [indicating that this is when he slept]*)*

The numbers one to six indicate the number of feeds. The notations which indicate a passage of time, for example 6.15–8 a.m., indicate how long Stephen was at the breast (unless they specify that he slept).

Every day until 27 December there is a record similar to the one above, sometimes with little additions. For example, on 13 December it mentions 'settled in MT at 9 a.m.'. MT stands for mytai, a kind of sling. There are references to the breast used on concluding a feed—'all on left breast', 'ended on right [breast]'. There are also references to vomiting and burping. Passing wind is difficult for babies, for some more than others. 'Winding' is a chore and an art. I spent hours trying to coax wind out of Stephen. People, including the nurse at the local weigh-in centre, used the word 'colic' to describe what was going on. It seems many babies have 'it'. But nobody could tell me just exactly what 'it' was or how to deal with it. I tried all the recommended remedies, including Gripe Water. Nothing helped.

The words 'settled', 'unsettled' and even 'resettled' dominate these early records. They are misleading words. They sound peaceful, even passive, suggesting a process that is easy and not traumatic. They conceal hours of patting and rocking. They conceal unbelievable fatigue. They conceal concern and indeed fear.

What was the purpose of these records? Why did I record these details? I think that it is probably unusual. There are several kinds of explanations. For one, I am an academic; records and schedules are second nature to me. This is an important point. In later reflections on the source/s of the difficulties I faced, I will consider seriously the suggestion that I, as an older first-time mother, had difficulty changing my ways, and that an older first-time mother who was an academic/professional faced particular challenges in this area. And I will consider seriously the suggestion that I was and continue to be ruled by schedules. But I want to insist that I do not necessarily see this as a part of me, as a part of my 'condition'. Rather I want to focus upon the *reasons* I wanted a schedule, the *reasons* I wanted predictability. The kind of busy lives we lead, complicated by holding down any kind of paid labour, made some degree of predictability essential. The lack of fit between the pressures to 'perform' on time and the inevitable variability and vicissitude associated with early childrearing is a central theme in this narrative.

The records also gave me a hold on reality. I was not getting enough sleep. Again, folk wisdom comforts new mothers and new parents with the adage that sleep deprivation is a form of torture. But adages don't help much. Thinking back, I can remember days, weeks, months without a solid night's sleep. I can remember feeling constantly tired. I remember wanting desperately to sleep but knowing that I couldn't. Stephen woke so frequently. He didn't start to sleep through the night, with any regularity, until he was almost two years old. And he had odd sleep patterns, waking almost predictably half-an-hour after he was settled for naps and for the night. So I would wait for him to wake. There seemed little point in allowing myself to get into a deep sleep only to be roused from it. Sometimes, when I did this, he broke the pattern and waited until midnight to wake. Babies like breaking patterns. This I learnt. So, I felt disoriented, yes even panicky and indeed tense. Lack of sleep can do that to you. Keeping records made it all seem real.

Chapter 3

Respite

There is a break in the Feeding Records between 28 December 1992 and 19 January 1993. Important things happened during this period. My brother and his wife came to visit from Brisbane. They found me 'not coping' and whisked Stephen and me away to their home in the north. My sister-in-law had a three year old at the time and she knew many things I needed to know. I sometimes think she saved our lives. But that sounds a little too dramatic, doesn't it? In fact, I think that I was very near breaking point.

Stephen continued to scream in his more tropical environment. We lived in one of those little self-enclosed suburbs where the streets circle back on themselves and there is very little traffic. I spent many mornings, from 4 a.m., walking up and down these streets, trying to get Stephen back to sleep. As I pushed his pram back and forth past squashed cane toads, I can remember being grateful that Queensland doesn't have daylight saving. All this would have been more difficult in the dark.

In typical suburban Queensland fashion, the neighbours would pop in to offer advice. After all, it was difficult to conceal what was going on. Stephen and I made quite a public spectacle on our morning hikes. And his high-pitched wails reverberated across the landscape. No one in the community was immune. Hence, I can certainly understand their desire to do something.

Janice lived next door. She had three children and you got the feeling that, whatever difficulty you were facing, she had already been there, done that. She had an earthy, warm manner, and a hearty laugh. In her view, it was fairly clear that Stephen wasn't sleeping because he was hungry. And his lack of enthusiasm at the breast was due to the fact that he wasn't getting much sustenance there. 'When are you going to put him on the bottle?' she asked.

My sister-in-law and I discussed this. It seemed too big a decision to take on our own. After all, she had successfully breastfed. And we had both read about all the good things breastfeeding did for mother and child. We had to think about bonding and immune systems. We decided that we needed advice. This took us to one of several clinics which offer exactly that—advice. They have a technique for estimating just how much milk the baby is taking. They weigh the baby before and then after the feed and tell you if things are going well. Stephen, it seems, was getting approximately 90 millilitres of milk at each feed. This, we were told, was all he needed. The fact that he was somewhat 'unsettled' was put down to 'colic', that explanation which said everything, and nothing.

So, it was back to pounding the pavement and wondering why this had to happen to me, wondering when things would change. Another week of sleepless nights and my sister-in-law pushed me into action. We ignored the advice of the clinic, purchased bottles and formula, and fed Stephen. He took 180 ml. at this first feed and slept for six hours. Janice popped her head in the door during this period and gloated, 'So, you finally put him on the bottle.'

Stephen was now six weeks old. I 'consoled' myself that we had made that first acceptable cut-off point for breastfeeding. Six weeks old is considered the earliest possible time to cease breastfeeding if you want the baby to absorb the benefits of your immune system. I expressed milk for a few days to get them used to the idea of unemployment, but there was little to express. My breasts almost looked relieved that they would no longer be asked to do something of which they were incapable.

I look back now and am angry that the first six weeks of mothering were such an unpleasant experience. I am angry that my poor little baby was hungry for the first six weeks of his life. I am angry that 90 ml. was considered 'adequate' and that I was sent away to cope with a screaming infant. You see, these first six weeks set up a pattern which was then difficult to break. Concluding, rightly or wrongly, that a good deal of Stephen's distressed state was due to hunger, I became determined that Stephen would never be hungry again. The key to our survival and my sanity seemed to be regular and adequate feeding. This, I believe, explains why I resumed the Feeding Records on 19 January 1993.

The first post-bottle record reads:

1. *1.20 a.m. (170 ml.)*
2. *5.30 a.m. (120 ml.)*
3. *8.15 (100 ml.)*
4. *11.30 (100 ml.)*
5. *3 p.m. (150 ml.)*
6. *9 p.m. (150 ml.)*

The colic hadn't gone away, however. Life did not slip into some version of the idealised chubby cheeked infant in glowing mother's arms. The records for the next three months are filled with references to 'positing' (that delightful little habit of regurgitating undigested milk) and 'winding'. On Sunday 24 January, 'we' had '2 great burps'; on Tuesday 26 January, at 10.15 a.m. there was 'wind'; at 5 p.m. the same day there was a 'strange reaction'.

Added to the feeding problems were the bowel problems. Stephen tended to get constipated. And so alongside the references to 'panet water', there are instructions for mixing Multagen. And alongside the references to wind and 'unsettled', there are records of 'b/o's. The whole exercise of mothering had turned into the management of one very tiny, very irritable digestive system. No one had warned me that this might happen.

On 28 January 1993 at 7.15 p.m. there is a record which states that Stephen had bowel problems and that a 'deep bath facilitated feed which had been rejected with screaming'. This is important because it indicates that there was evidence of food rejection before I can remember it happening. As you will see, in March of 1993 Stephen became quite ill. I thought that our problems began then; I was convinced of it. That's the way I remember it happening. In effect, however, it seems that our problems only became *worse* after his illness. It seems that we had problems before this. The records tell a tale I don't recall. They indicate to me that from the outset feeding Stephen was a preoccupation, that I wanted it to go smoothly.

The records also show that the difficulties of 'colic' and 'constipation' were accompanied by the many other things which happen to babies. There is a reference to a cold, and to a fever. These events did not make mothering easier. They meant more references to 'unsettled' and more broken nights.

On Wednesday 3 February, there is a reference to a CAFHS (Child and Family Health Services) visit. This is one of those little local clinics which weighs your baby and lets you know how he is going (i.e. growing). They also offer a shoulder for weary mothers to cry on. The nurse on duty said that she thought Stephen might have reflux. She also told me (and it is written in my Diary in extra large letters), 'MUST HAVE 5 FEEDS A DAY. WAKE IF NECESSARY'. And so this was the regime I instituted. Looking back, I feel that I was so naive and gullible that I accepted anyone's advice. Actually, I think I was a little more like that proverbial drowning sailor who would grab onto any life buoy tossed my way. Wednesday 3 February 7.45 p.m. also has the first reference to 'reflux'. It wouldn't be the last. It is at this time that Stephen began rejecting his food with great determination, pushing away his bottles and screaming in distress. He was two months old.

Chapter 4

Getting it Together

Reflux, it seems to me, is what they call colic when colic doesn't go away. I realise that this is simplistic but I'm afraid that I was never offered a better explanation. Reflux, it seems, is a form of heartburn, which is indigestion with a capital 'I'. There is a muscle located at the bottom of the oesophagus which opens to let food in and closes to keep food in the stomach. When this muscle relaxes for too long or too often, stomach acid shoots up the oesophagus. Very unpleasant! I'm one of those lucky people who had never had heartburn until I was pregnant. And when it happened I thought that I was having a heart attack. Very unpleasant indeed!

I never had the energy at the time to research reflux. I suppose it isn't odd that the sicker we are, the more we tend to rely on doctors' advice. The reasons are twofold: one, we are too busy coping with the 'symptoms' to research the causes; second, we need reassurance and take it in any form. This, anyway, is how I responded to the talk of 'reflux'. I was pleased because I had a name for a problem I couldn't handle. And, with a diagnosis, there are usually 'remedies'. These were offered in due course.

When I decided to write this memoir, I had a look on the net to see what there was about reflux. The Children's Medical Centre of Dallas described GERD

(Gastroesophagea Reflux Disease) in some detail.[2] One common symptom, it seems, and this should not be surprising, is 'refusal to feed'. No one ever told me this. I struggled with the symptoms more or less on my own.

By early February some new kinds of entries are appearing in the Feeding Records. On 4 February at the 3.30 a.m. feed, I wrote 'reflux?'. At 7.30 p.m. that day, I wrote 'no attack'. On 10 February at 5.25 p.m., I wrote '220 ml—attack'. On 16 February at the 4.25 a.m. feed, I wrote 'cried out in pain'. The change in language could have been due to the CAFHS nurse's suggestion that Stephen had a 'condition', something called 'reflux', with symptoms. On the other hand, her description of the 'problem' might simply have provided me with a more accurate way of describing what was happening. I mean, how does a mother describe food rejection? We don't have any commonly accepted ways of describing this in infants, do we? Infants are supposed to feed, and feed enthusiastically. Then they are supposed to 'sleep like babies'. Stephen wasn't doing either.

We have come up with a language for describing food rejection later in life. We call the 'illness'

---

2   See http://www.childrens.com/heathin/Display.efm?ID=793&main=777 Accessed 10 October 2001.

'anorexia nervosa' and there are numerous attempts to explain its occurrence. In my recent foray onto the web there were references to 'infantile anorexia' but there was concern about this language. This is because teen anorexia is often attributed to complex socialisation patterns, patterns you wouldn't expect in a toddler and certainly not in an infant. There are similar debates about the inadequacy of labelling feeding disorders in infants 'NOFTT' (Failure to Thrive) on the grounds that this is more of a *description* of what is happening than an *explanation*.[3]

In the realm of explanation, feeding disorders are most frequently seen as 'transactional disorders', some breakdown in the maternal-infant feeding interactions.[4] While this focus sounded promising to me since it is indeed mother-child interactions which I want to emphasise, I was disturbed by the way in which some accounts tended to blame the mother. In one article, for example, key 'broken' interactions

---

3   Irene Chatoor (1998) 'Diagnosing infantile anorexia: the observation of mother-infant interactions', *Journal of the American Academy of Child and Adolescent Psychiatry,* September.

4   L. Lindberg, G. Bohlin, B. Hagekull & K. Palmerus (1996) 'Interactions between mothers and infants showing food refusal', *Journal of Infant Mental Health,* 17: 334-347.

were 'overt hostility' and 'allowing the baby to sleep through feedings'.[5] I actually have some sympathy with both of these reactions. Who wouldn't be angry if they were exhausted and a screaming child pushed away the bottle? Who wouldn't allow a child to sleep if they didn't tend to do this all that much? I turn to the Diaries to explore the nature of my interactions with Stephen.

We returned from Brisbane to Canberra on 11 February 1993. I was feeling that the worst was over. Stephen, now ten weeks old, was on the bottle and hence was feeding better. But feeding was still not a pleasant experience for him or for me.

17 February 1993   Settling into Canberra. A few break-throughs today. Gripe water seemed to help greatly with winding. Also, bath time was a success—in the little bath. Timing crucial—one hour or so after afternoon feed.

18 Feb   My God, this winding is hard work. I still hate to see him cry. There must be an easier way. All in good time, I suppose.

---

5   C. Haynes, C. Cutler, J. Gray & R. Kempe (1984)
     'Hospitalized cases of nonorganic failure to thrive', *Child Abuse and Neglect*, 8: 229–242.

19 Feb And now we wait for a bowel motion. Stephen still in good form as we lead up to the 4 p.m. feed.

First swim at the Institute pool. Feeling weary, but good about it. I love to be in the water.

The house is in good shape. And things are looking better every day.

It was time, I concluded, to return to my original plan to be back on the job after three months maternity leave. I started Stephen in childcare and recommenced my (paid) work. At the time I was holding a research-only position which gave me the kind of flexibility I needed to combine paid work and childrearing as a single parent, or so I believed. I had checked out childcare centres and they looked fine. Of course, I had nothing with which to compare them; they were the first I'd seen. The following entries provide glimpses into the challenge of bringing together (paid) work and infant care.

Tuesday 23rd Feb.   Took Stephen into the office today where he was a great hit—in good form, smiling—a real charmer.

Held his first rattle today and definitely knew what he was doing.

The pram where he could see me worked. The capsule was also a success. Real headway being made.

I feel weary today—not sure why. Probably because I'm trying to monitor his night feeds—to encourage him to feed to suit my day-time schedules. This keeps my sleep close to the surface.

24 Feb./93   Slept in a cot for the first time last night. Looked adorable in his snuggle bag. Woke early (3.15 a.m.) for a feed and again at 7.15—changes schedule for whole day. Picked up mail in office—time to face the <u>other</u> real world.

25 Feb.   A difficult day today. Seemed to have an upset tummy—passed a lot of wind. Left me feeling tense & a touch negative about things. Passed quickly.

26 Feb.   All smiles this morning. Still having trouble reading his night-time behaviours. Awoke at 3 a.m. bright eyed & bushy tailed—but hungry. Still he didn't cry out for a bottle. He was certainly ready at 7.15 a.m. this morning & hence has rearranged the day for me—to suit his feeds. Had great success with winding this morning & he had a good bowel movement, on schedule, without straining.

1st March /Monday   [Stephen is three months old.] *First day back at the office.*

Friday 5 March   Where has the week gone? I'm quite pleased really. I've done some reading and begun to think again. I've also managed a few swims—a little time for myself. Stephen is settling down in many ways. He seems less easily distressed. He is also reorganising his feeding schedule which is OK so long as I go to bed shortly after he does. This has been getting earlier & earlier, however (8 p.m. last night). It will be good when some pattern is established . . .

I keep thinking that I should be recording more than mundane events, but there is little time for reflection. Generally, I'm <u>very</u> happy with the change Stephen has made in my life. He's added a new dimension, a new texture—and he makes me laugh! Just thinking of his little smile makes me smile.

I do feel a little guilty about the hours he's in childcare— mainly because he's in a room of toddlers & this restricts his freedom of movement. Still, I believe the sensory stimulation he is receiving there is more than I could provide at home. He is also getting used to new people, activities all around him & sounds. This must be preferable to growing up in the cocoon of a single quiet dwelling with one caretaker.

I could, of course, allow you to make your own judgments about these excerpts, but I can't help feeling that a psychologist would have a field-day with them, identifying my need for predictability and order. Hence, I feel that I need to say something. With hindsight, I am deeply distressed to see how I was trying to manage my life (our lives). I kept wanting things to become predictable so that I could get on with my (paid) work. This, of course, had been my original plan, and I have never liked changes imposed on my plans. But there is another angle which needs comment and exploring. The simple point I want to make is that Stephen *had* to become predictable to fit in with the normal day-to-day routine of working life. Recall here that my work regime was more flexible than most. Still, there was an expectation that I would accomplish a set amount in a certain time. I was being paid to do this. So, I ask you, which came first—my obsession with making Stephen fit a schedule, or the kind of regulated, time-obsessed lives most of us live?

Monday 8 March   My first blue day—actually a fairly blue weekend. The cause—Stephen's feeds have become completely unpredictable. It started with a 140 ml. feed on Saturday morning (he usually takes 180 ml.). I thought this an aberration but he had poor feeds almost all weekend & this morning he took only 110 ml. I'm not sure what's happening. He looks healthy enough & he's certainly hungry when I feed him. The feeds are also a little close together which would explain the drops in volume. I suppose it's the uncertainty which troubles me. I'm not good at dealing with uncertainty but I'll have to improve . . .

13 March/93   Election day. Ended last night in tears—another small feed (I enforced 120 ml. & faced the overflow). I must learn to wait for him to demand the bottle. Last night I woke him hoping to encourage a particular pattern of feeding & it didn't work. Let's face it, Carol—over this you have no control. Something like your bowels—you'll have to wait for them to move!

Chapter 5

Falling Apart

There are no entries for 14 and 15 March. This is because Stephen became very ill and I was desperately trying to find out what was wrong. One locum sent me home, telling me all he needed was a little Panadol. A more thorough locum called me to the examination table and asked me to look into Stephen's throat as he shone a torch. Stephen's little mouth and throat were covered with what looked like mouth ulcers. I was sent home with antibiotics. But Stephen's temperature continued to climb. A friend came over at 3 a.m. and we took Stephen into the emergency ward at the local hospital.

I will always remember standing a little off to one side as doctors and nurses milled around Stephen, whispering in what sounded to be very worried tones. I heard the word 'meningitis' and I felt that my heart stopped. I wasn't quite sure what meningitis involved but I knew it was serious. I was terrified that I was losing Stephen. My state was worse than panic. I hadn't slept in some time and had trouble concentrating. I think that I was losing hope; I felt defeated.

In the event, Stephen, now three-and-a-half months old, was diagnosed with viral pharangytis and admitted for a few days. He needed penicillin in quite large doses and careful monitoring for fluid intake. I was offered and took the option of a bed in the parents' quarters. I wanted to be close by, even if it meant that I would sleep even less than usual. I just couldn't leave Stephen alone in that God-awful place.

16 March/93   How do I feel? Not bad considering. I suppose I feed [sic; as in original] *I can handle—. . . he's proving difficult to put to sleep . . . He's really quite unsettled—but it's noisy & there are babies crying. The important thing is that I'm here—and **I** can settle him. At least I won't let him scream. It's a strange place to be. And I feel that Stephen and I are at the bottom of the barrel. There are asthma attacks & unknown illnesses— and no one notices Stephen. I have really got to get him out of here.*

My work is on hold. My life is on hold. I have nothing on my mind but Stephen—and a little sleep for me perhaps.

17 March/93   I didn't sleep much—despite the Jim Beam. I asked the staff to wake me for his feed but they didn't. I lay awake waiting for the call.

This morning Stephen was congested and I panicked. Now he's playing happily. Unfortunately he's still not feeding well.

Thursday 18 March/93   Now Stephen has nappy rash, is shitting liquid and still has a sore mouth. But it's time to go home—when it comes to it, there's little more they can do for us here.

I managed to get him to take 180 ml. this morning (he was quite warm)—without Panadol. It just takes persistence and <u>PATIENCE</u>.

While I was scanning the internet on infant feeding disorders (refusal) I came across something referred to as 'post-traumatic feeding disorder.'[6] I had never heard of this before. I now wonder why someone did not predict that, given Stephen's history and the concerns about reflux, that feeding just might become an even more difficult thing when he had a very, very sore throat. But no one did. With hindsight, it now makes sense to me that for Stephen eating was a mixed blessing. Yes, it satisfied that thing we call hunger pangs and that was good, but it hurt and that was bad. And so he would scream for food, the way all infants are wont to do, but then he would push away the bottle and scream even more loudly. I was left alone to deal with this situation.

I have been pondering just why feeding assumed the critical importance it did in my relationship with

---

6   D. Benoit & J. Coolbear (1998) 'Post-traumatic feeding disorders in infancy', *Journal of Infant Mental Health,* 19(4): 409-21.

Stephen. This topic comes up again later, when I am forced (by myself) to seek 'professional help'. At this stage I think my main concern was keeping him quiet. I needed peace and sleep. His cries tore my soul apart. It sounded as if he were starving. Now, I know that this sounds ridiculous but it would have helped had someone said quite simply that he wasn't starving, that he would live. So, was my reaction due to lack of experience? Was my intolerance to my baby's cry due to my being an older first-time mother?

Maybe. But there were other factors. I mentioned the 'weigh-in' clinics (CAFHS). These helpful services can have some detrimental effects. I was told often that Stephen wasn't gaining enough weight. 'What was enough weight?', I wanted to ask. But I didn't. Typically, I deferred to professionals. You would have thought that, being a professional myself of sorts, I would have had less, not more respect for them, but I didn't. I usually took their 'words of wisdom' seriously. I concluded that I had to fatten Stephen up. The obsession with feeding him was heightened.

18 March/93   Home by 12.30–noon. What a relief!

19 March/ Friday   Got through the night. Really difficult feed this morning. Managed to get 90 ml. into him using Panadol.

Sunday 22March   Things on the improve. I'm using Panadol for the morning and evening feeds—partly for my sanity. Other feeds are difficult but we're getting there. Stephen is sleeping much better and has more energy. Consequently so does Mum.

Monday 23 March   Got through the weekend though it was long. Stephen seems to be switching to a three-hour feeding regime. In a way this is quite OK since it reduces his crotchety time. Maybe this is what he always wanted.

Tues 24 March   Things going much better since I accepted Stephen's preference for smaller, more frequent feeds. I have even been able to manipulate his schedule to give myself a decent night's sleep. I still sleep close to the surface, however, wondering when 'my master's voice' will ring out!

Feeding Record:

Fri 19/3 at home
1.   *1 a.m. (140 ml. without Panadol)*
2.   *6.30 (90 ml. with Pan.)*
      7 a.m. (loose motion)
      Gel + cream (for nappy rash)
3.   *10   110 ml. Pan.*
4.   *1.15   140 ml. Panadol*
5.   *4.15   120 ml.*
      Gel + cream
6.   *8.15 (180 ml.—gave .8 ml Pan at 7.15)*

Sun 21/3/93

1. *3.45 a.m. (150 ml.)*
    (loose motion—7.30 a.m.)
    7.15—6 ml Panadol. Cream.
2. *8 a.m. (160 ml. after a break) Gel.*
3. *11.20 a.m. (180 ml without trauma or Panadol. Crying at beginning/needs soothing)*
4. *3.05 (145 ml.)*
5. *6.15 (145 ml)*
6. *9.10 (120 ml)*

Carefully totalled at the bottom of the sheet: *150+160+180+290+120=900*

Tues 24 March (continued)
It [i.e. my master's voice] *rang out & then a bad feed. Turned his head from the bottle almost immediately. Eventually took 145 ml. but I can't understand what the problem was. Was the throat sore? Should I have fed him immediately upon waking?*

25 March/93   Wednesday, I think. Stephen rearranged the night for me last night. Just when I thought I could count on his 'long' sleep, he called for a feed at 1 A.M., followed by another at 5.45 A.M. Both were smallish, 150 and 135 mls. Happily he went back to sleep at 6 A.M. I'm now waiting to see what happens next.

Chapter 6

Coping—Not!

The pattern of smallish feeds and refusals continued for the following couple of weeks. My life revolved around getting Stephen to consume a 'decent' amount of milk each day. The Diaries record my efforts to find help in conventional and in non-traditional quarters. The Feeding Records capture the daily agony and stress I faced. They also mention the techniques I had developed to deal with the 'problem'. Looking back, much of this surprised me. In my head I started using 'tricks'—such as warm baths to relax him, playing his musical mobile, distracting him with toys, laying him on a tripillow (a V-shaped pillow) instead of holding him—to get Stephen to feed only after the forced feeding episode in the Mothers' Hospital (17 May 1993; see Chapter 1). In fact, I have a little story that I tell people about how I discovered that I had to use distraction during our final stay in the Mothers' Hospital (21 to 25 May). The story goes that I passed by Stephen who was sitting in a nursery playpen, leaned over to offer him a bottle and dangled a toy in the other hand. The story goes that he took the bottle and that I was overjoyed. The story goes that this then became the key to coping. The Diaries and Feeding Records tell a different story and I sometimes wonder where I was during this period in my life with Stephen.

Feeding Records (excerpts):

Thurs 25/3 2.40 a.m. (*170 ml. Took head away several times but was still hungry/lay him down/rewarmed milk. 6.30 a.m. (with Panadol. 120 ml. Great effort).*

Tues. 30/3/93 6.45 a.m. (*gave Panadol/he had a nap/not hungry by 7.30 am). 8 a.m. (with bath—70 ml.)*

Wed. 31 March. 5.30 a.m (*90 ml. on waking/ no protest till I offered more). 9.30 a.m. (180 ml. At clinic after initial refusal) 3.40 pm. Sometimes resists later in feed. Draws up legs. 7.30 p.m. spilling up clear liquid.*

Fri. 2/4/93. 6.45 am. [Stephen is four months old.] *Tried holding him to guarantee sleep from 5.45 am. Then added a little Multagen since no b/o. Tried on pillow. Pushed away bottle.*

Sat 3/4 2–2.45 a.m. 200 ml. + first rice cereal [beginning of solids]. *Protested. Stopped at 80 ml. Finished on tripillow. Used tripillow + BABAR* [musical mobile] *for second half.*

Diary entries (excerpts):

Sat. 27th March. A weekend—let's see how I cope. Must learn to relax about feeds. If he doesn't get hysterical for childcare staff, there's no reason for it to happen with me. And it didn't in hospital or the other night at dinner.

Monday 29th March.   Got thru the weekend. Waited till he cried for his morning feed—still turned his head away. An ordeal. Tomorrow I'll try to comfort him. Maybe I just presumed the cry was hunger. But he seems to want the bottle. I'm confused!

Tues. 30th March.   Got thru the night. Stephen had a disaster of a day at childcare. Wouldn't feed till he produced a huge burp.

Wed. 31st March.   This morning we're off to a Family Care Clinic (FCC) to see if someone can help Stephen with his feeding disorder. [First time I use this phrase in the Diaries]. *I still face the morning feed with trepidation. Yesterday the childcare people had similar trouble (rejection) with other feeds.*

I'm now up at 5 a.m. to get the bottles made before he rises. I'm also taking laxatives again to guarantee a strain-free motion—the piles are quite serious right now (as if piles could be anything else!)

I've included the above entry to show that there was another person, another body, involved in this drama. Here I am, some four months after Stephen's birth, and I am *still* suffering with piles.

Thurs 1 April/93.   The clinic 'narrowed' the problem down—it's either physical or psychological. Actually I think there may be two separate problems—one which causes the initial rejection & the other causing Stephen to come off the bottle early. The first, I believe, is a residue of pain caused by the throat infection. The second could be a form of reflux—it is certainly related to trapped wind or wind rising. Must check with Dr Jones about this.

Re-think. He definitely sucks differently (less smoothly) when he is wide awake & hence takes in wind which puts him off the bottle. That is, unless he is <u>really</u> hungry . . . or relaxed. The danger in waiting until he's really hungry is that he will become overwrought & reject the bottle from the outset <u>or</u> become overwrought & hence take in wind when he tries to drink. So he needs to be hungry (but not too hungry) & calm. Timing is crucial. It may also be possible to reduce the wind intake with a change of teat. Today we'll try silicon orthodontic—here goes nothing.

Fri. 2/4/93. Tried everything this morning—pillow, bath—he just wasn't interested.

Sun. 4/4/93. Yesterday made ground at Janice and Mark's. The tripillow worked—after a disastrous start to a feed. The key is to make feeding a pleasure & not to be so upset about intake. I'm trying to get Stephen into the Mothers' Hospital. They claim they can teach him to sleep during the day. They also say they can increase his feeds. If Janice hadn't endorsed the place, I'd be highly suspicious. I've also decided to keep him out of childcare till after Easter. Perhaps the noise & everything was just too much after the illness. I hope it's not a permanent aversion. I couldn't afford a full-time nanny.

Chapter 7

Mothers and Babies

The episode related in Chapter 1 tells of my third visit to the Mothers' Hospital. The first occurred in early April and is described below. Stephen was four months old.

These hospitals can give desperate mothers/parents a break and, as you will see, I was grateful for some respite. But, as you will also see, I felt an odd adversarial relationship with the nursing staff, almost as if they received a perverse pleasure from proving themselves right and me wrong. This might have been an idiosyncratic experience. I have no way of knowing.

It is also possible that *I* was the one who created the adversarial relationship. After all, admission to one of these hospitals is almost an admission (interesting that the word is the same) that you, the parent, are doing something wrong—unless you have cracked nipples, of course. Oh, for some cracked nipples! So, it is possible that I felt on the defensive from the outset. If this is the case, then perhaps the problem is the expectation that mothering/parenting is easy, the expectation that things *should* go smoothly. If we could accept that mothering/parenting can be excruciatingly difficult, then perhaps the pressure to be perfect would not exist. It would follow that seeking help is no indication of failure.

On this, the first stay in the Mothers' Hospital, they kept Stephen for three nights. I was allowed to go home.

Tuesday 6 April/93
Stephen was admitted to the Mothers' Hospital—a hospital for babies with 'problems'—this morning. Should I feel a failure? I don't think so since things really only started to go wrong after the throat infection—i.e. bottle rejection, small feeds, short sleeps. Should I feel guilty because I needed help? Not really. I could have handled it. We were on the improve but why not use help if it's available. Should I feel guilty about a sense of release I feel? Not really. I haven't had a breather in weeks & the nights have been hell.

Thursday 8 April/93
Two good nights sleep & the body is in shock. Don't know how long they'll keep Stephen but it can't be much longer. He's doing really well—downing his bottles and rice cereal (for latter mix extra formula & warm/keep sloppy). The Dr saw him and recommended Mylanta (1 m. or 2.5 m.) for indigestion + suppository for constipation (like mother, like son). They've also imposed a new sleep regime—at least an hour between feeds (possibly an hour and a half). Stephen is to be tucked tightly into his cot and patted off. I did it last night & he protested only briefly. Seems once he's been up one and a half or two hours, he <u>needs</u> sleep.

47

Most significant. Though I needed a break, I miss him terribly. I suddenly realised just how empty my life has become when he's not around. Life is easier—can't say I miss mixing formula—but who wants to spend all her time reading feminist theory. Stephen & I have such good times to come!

Friday 9th April 1993
A disappointment this morning. They decided to keep Stephen another day. And I know it was because I displayed such a lack of confidence when the morning feed didn't go well . . . He comes home tomorrow!

Sat. 10th April (early A.M.)
Why am I feeling slightly daunted this morning? I suppose it's because I realise just how <u>alone</u> I am in all this. I ran over the check list of who is in town over the next few days & practically drew a blank. I also realise that it is time for Stephen & me to start negotiating space & time. I can no longer treat him like a thing, to be rocked off to sleep, etc. I have to let him know what is expected of him . . .

Stephen is home and I'm sitting here waiting for him to wake for a feed!

Sunday. Easter. 11 April/93
A dream morning. Fed Stephen last night around 7 p.m. at Janice and Mark's. They tried to feed him & it was not working so I intervened. Stephen took 180 ml. + stewed

pear. Took him home & patted him off around 8.15 p.m.
He might have slept through but I worried about his milk
intake—he had had only 4 bottles (760 ml.) yesterday—
so when he stirred at 2.15 a.m. I fed him (180 ml.) . . .
Same day—P.M.—and so the new regime continues.
Fiona [childcare person who helped me at home] *had*
little success feeding Stephen and so I finished him on
the pillow—but got a full bottle into him + 2 tsp cereal +
2 tsp pear + another 40 ml. milk.

Several important patterns can be seen in the
Diaries at this stage. First, fewer and fewer people
could feed Stephen. In fact, it is fair to say that by
this stage he would accept food only from me (with
the exception of nursing staff who 'had their ways';
see Chapter 1). This meant that I had to be there for
all his feeds. In addition, because Stephen was so
easily distracted and because I had developed
unconventional techniques to get him to take a
bottle, including lying him on a tripillow (see
above), feeds had to be given at home. I needed a
quiet place to 'administer' feeds. When we put these
conditions for 'success' together with the increasing
unpredictability of Stephen's feeds, the result was
that I had smaller and smaller windows of opportunity to leave the house. This was whether I was
alone or with Stephen. Whenever we went out, I had

to have one eye on my watch to make sure we were back in time for his feed.

I was still trying to get to my paid work at this stage, but the pressure was beginning to show. Again, I want to note how unpredictability around feeding clashed with the expectation that I would be in a certain place at a certain time. My guess is that my obsession with establishing a routine tied into the expectation that I could keep one. I also needed to find some way to get more sleep. I couldn't 'function' on what I was getting.

Tuesday 13th April 1993   I know it's too soon but a potential pattern—the early waking pattern—seems to be emerging. Eventually I'd try to get the last feed around 7 p.m. & eventually Stephen would skip the 2 a.m. feed. I hope this isn't too much to hope for.

Food Record (excerpt): *2 a.m. (190 ml.) I woke him concerned re the 2.30 p.m. feed which would make it possible for me to attend the seminar.*

Diary: *Friday 16 April/93   I turn 45 tomorrow—a note in case I'm too busy to make comment. A very difficult couple of days. I've been attending a conference Thurs. & Fri. and Stephen seemed unable to settle both Wednesday night & last night . . . Don't know how I keep functioning on so little sleep.*

Chapter 8

Rock-a-bye Baby

The trips to the Mothers' Hospital had almost as much to do with sleep as they did with food. 'Controlled crying' was in vogue and I did my best to implement it, but I wasn't very good at it. I found it physically painful to hear Stephen cry. I had my own technique for getting him to sleep. The Diaries refer to it as 'rocking him off'. It involved holding him and swivelling my whole body as if I were rotating a hula-hoop until he fell asleep. This could take as much as twenty or thirty minutes, but eventually it would work. I sometimes thought that I was making him so dizzy that he just passed out. And it was quite a workout—I got very thin during this period. Needless to say, this was not a technique looked upon favorably by hospital staff. Stephen was now four-and-a-half months old.

Sat. 17 April/93   Last night began in agony. Allowed Stephen three bouts of crying (1 minute, 2 then 3) to get to sleep. Finally rocked him off a little. He woke every two hours & except for the 2 a.m. feed, I managed to resist going into him. I lay in bed and counted to one hundred. Thank God, he stopped crying before I reached the end.

Things clearly were not going well. And so, it should come as no surprise that I was forced to return to the Mothers' Hospital. I became desperate for help.

18 April 2 a.m.   Defeat. He's back in the Mothers' Hospital.

They kept Stephen until 21 April, four nights if we include the arrival at 2 a.m. on 18 April. The Diaries tell a story of confusion and increasing distress.

Monday 19th April 93.   Another day. The beginning of another week. Hope it's better than the last. Slept fairly well, though I've been awake on & off since 4 a.m. Skipped the sleeping pills—hit the Scotch. Thought I'd function better. Miss Stephen terribly. Must sort out a few things today. Must find out what they're doing re controlled crying. If the problem is physical, why are we using behaviour modification techniques? Stephen is becoming terrified of a cot. Should I bring him home? . . . Ultrasound produced no findings (thankfully). Tomorrow it's X-rays and the test for reflux.

20 April/93   Slept like a log last night. First deep sleep in months, it seems. Body is shell-shocked.

21 April/93   I'm bringing Stephen home this morning, regardless of what the tests show. Yesterday I was away for just an hour & returned to find him in a state. They were about to feed him, though he wasn't due for an hour & a half. The sister Belinda makes me feel a fool— keeps saying there's nothing wrong with Stephen except a little cold. She's probably right, but the way she says it leaves me feeling very inadequate. She also suggested that they'd be seeing me again. Not if I can help it—I assure you!

In the event, I couldn't help it and Belinda proved right. But I struggled to deal with the 'problem' for another three weeks before I gave in again. During this period I made important decisions about my paid work.

21 April (continued)   He's home—and now I have to administer something for the reflux & antibiotics for the cold (for 10 days, twice daily). I need a little practice slipping the syringe into his mouth. Fiona's been with me most of the day & with two people everything seems easy . . . Tomorrow is Thursday & I'll go into the office to clear up a few things—the summary on sexuality and the paragraph on affirmative action.

Friday 23 April/93   Stephen had a very disturbed night again last night. It must be the cold [his cold] *which is waking him. I erred and offered him a bottle he didn't want at 3 a.m. He wasn't hungry again at 7.30 this morning. He's still consuming enough but he's definitely on the slight side. I felt unhappy about the antibiotics which had been prescribed. Had Stephen checked by another GP today who agreed they were unnecessary.*

Sat 24/4/93   Today the cold was worse. Back to the doctor & now he's on antibiotics (Septrin & Demazin for congestion). This is in addition to the Otrivin nose drops & Panadol (as needed!).

Food Record: *Sat 24/4/93 7.15 a.m. (160 ml. used every trick in the book).*

Sun 25/4/93   I've more or less decided that I need to take a few months off (long service leave) to get on top of things. The nights continue to be unpredictable (as do the days).

Tuesday 27/4/93   Seems I'll be able to delay the Canada [research] *trip & I don't expect any problems extending the deadline with the publishers. In fact, I feel I can breathe more easily today.*

The pressures of my job exist as a backdrop to this drama. The Diaries reveal my repeated attempts to meet the intensely conflicting demands of 'paid work', as it is currently organised, and 'domestic responsibilities'.

The references to ultrasound and reflux tests above indicate that Stephen's physical problems were being taken seriously. He was even given an EEG. For this, he needed to fast four hours from 6 a.m. I plotted the whole night to make sure that we could handle this. Diary entry—*'in the end he took 140 ml.'* None of the tests revealed anything. I was beginning to conclude that the 'problem' was psychological and that I was the cause. But I hadn't quite yet given up on physiological explanations. And I continued to find ways to get Stephen to eat.

Food Record: *Thurs 29/4/93—12.30 chiropractor*

Diary: *29 April /93   Booked the immunisation and the visit to the naturopath next week. Then I'll see about baby massage.*

Food Record: *Thurs 29/4/93. 3 p.m. (220 ml. Goat's milk).*

Diary: *29 April/93   Tomorrow I'll write the letters clearing the deck of (paid) work . . . Now I'll have time to read a little on child development & help Stephen through some transitions—solids, sitting up, first teeth. He still 'squawks', as Fiona puts it, with some regularity. But I'm having an easier time bedding him down. I allow him to lie on his back & I stroke his brow & sing. He doesn't protest the way he used to.*

Last night he slept soundly from 5.45 p.m. Had to wake him for a bottle at 8.30 p.m. Woke at midnight. Then I resettled him & he called for a bottle at 2 a.m. After that he couldn't settle—seemed distressed. I gave him a shot of Panadol. Tonight I'll spend more effort on winding and could try the Mylanta. If indigestion is the problem, this might help.

I don't mind next to sleepless nights so long as I know I can count on a nap the next day when he's in childcare & so long as I don't have to accomplish anything.

And we seemed to be making some progress.

Sat. 1st May/93
A great day at the Edwards. I am astounded at how Stephen has turned into a little person over night. He was positively charming today, and this evening he chuckled heartily at Sally's antics . . . I can't believe all these changes are due to chiropractic & goat's milk!

Mon 3 May /93 . . . I wonder if there's any need for the naturopath on Wednesday. Things seem to have settled down beautifully.

Occasionally the mixed multitude of reasons for my concerns seep through. In a later entry I note that one of the many doctors we saw told me that Stephen needed a minimum of 300 ml. a day or he would become dehydrated. He never explained what would follow from this. But it sounded terrible. I had visions of Stephen drying up like a prune. To prevent this I found myself waking Stephen from 'long sleeps'. The management of feeds worked against sleep management. There were contradictions all over the place. Stephen was now five months old.

Tues 4 May /93   Spent the night worrying that Stephen was dehydrated because I had mixed the new goat's milk formula too strong. I find it very difficult to fill the scoop lightly given the formula's viscous texture. I was also concerned that he had cut back to four feeds, and yesterday threatened to go the night on three (I woke him at 10.30 p.m.). This plus the long sleeps (yesterday had to wake him from a two-hour 'nap' to bring him home from childcare) convinced me he was getting too many calories per bottle. I made an extra effort to fill the scoop lightly this morning. His bowel motion was weird again—a small dark brown turd followed by a loose yellowish mixture.

Clearly we were not out of the woods yet. And I continued to look for explanations.

Fri 7 May/93   Continuing to have trouble with feeds. Stephen sends out 'hungry' messages & then changes his mind. I then try to change it back . . . Been thinking about the feeding problem—Fiona's comment re huge burps + 2 episodes now where milk has come back. It is just possible that in my endeavours to make things easy [for Stephen to consume milk], *I have had the cap* [teat] *on the bottle too <u>loosely</u> so the milk comes too quickly & Stephen gulps air. Hence, when he pulls his head away he needs winding* [must have felt a little like drowning?!] *& there's no point in proceeding until the winding occurs. I feel terrible that I am inadvertently* *the cause of his problem, though it doesn't explain why he cries taking solids.*

8 May (Sat)   Now after several very soft bowel motions, it seems clear that Stephen has a tummy wog of some sort. Yesterday barely managed to get 600 ml. into him. I remember Dr Phelps saying 300 ml. is critical for dehydration. Today I'm satisfied if he drinks at all! . . . I've also switched to the Karicare cow-based formula. He kept spitting up the goat's milk and it stank. Couldn't help thinking that, if it repulsed me, it may also repulse him.

Sunday 9 May/93   Started the day very depressed. After the woman (sister) at the Mothers' Hospital told me Stephen's loose bowels were due to lack of food, I plotted all night how to get more into him. I woke him at midnight & he took only 110 ml. I worried & he tossed & turned the rest of the night. In the morning he just wouldn't take a decent feed despite every trick in the book. I felt defeated until the Edwards rescued me for Mothers' Day lunch & showed me yet again what an easy baby he is and how I need to loosen up. I bought a small booklet on Janice's advice in which to record all the good things that happen. I feel that this [the Diaries] *is a fairly balanced account but maybe I do accentuate the negative.*

The Food Records show that I was becoming more adept at distraction techniques. These, of course, indicate that feeding was continuing to be a real problem. What the Records can't show and what even the Diaries fail to capture is the growing tension inside me. I was still getting too little undisrupted sleep. My life had become an obsession with getting Stephen to feed. My days and nights were filled with fear of food rejection. No one, at least no one who hasn't experienced it, can understand the desperation produced when your baby cries with hunger and then pushes the bottle or spoon away, or simply cries with distress when you offer him food. The Food Records tell a story of escalating difficulties. The Diaries reveal growing desperation. My options were becoming fewer and fewer.

Food Record: *Mon 10/5/93 12 noon (160 ml. New trick. Letting him hold rattle) . . . 7.30 p.m.(180 ml. Shake rattle in right, hold bottle in left. Wind more than once. Snap fingers on left hand.)*

11 May Tues. Stephen slept from 8.30 p.m. to 8.30 a.m. I woke several times, convinced he was starving. Even prepared a bottle at 3.30 a.m. . . . Trauma at childcare yesterday when I found him stuck in a bouncinette crying his eyes out. I know things will improve when Diane is back next week but she goes on maternity leave in July.

Hence I'm putting out feelers for a nanny. But I need someone to share with to make it affordable. I want Stephen to have contact with other people but he needs more quiet to sleep and more space to explore his own mobility.

12 May/Wed. I keep writing down the 'good things' in my 'good vibes' notebook & there are plenty of them. Generally Stephen is happy. He seldom cries & then usually for a good reason. But all day what is on my mind is that he is off his food—formula <u>and</u> solids—and that he has stopped gaining weight. Yesterday he took only 650 ml. (and for that I had to wake him at 10 p.m. when he took only 100 ml.) He just doesn't seem hungry. The clinic sister says to take one week at a time but surely something's got to give. He isn't getting enough nutrition & no one seems to know why he isn't hungry!

Food Record: *Thurs 13/5/93 10.15 p.m. (180 ml.) Would have been disaster with other teat . . . He cut off after 70 or 80 ml. and started to cry when I persisted. Only the toy soldier worked. Problem is more psychological than physiological—need a more permanent solution.*

Diary: *13 May/Thurs. A few disastrous feeds. Can't figure out what is happening. Have spent the whole day around the flat waiting for Stephen to get hungry. Broke down for the first time and had a good cry . . . Must come to terms with this. My reaction is out of sync with the problem. Stephen is not going to die of starvation, nor will he dehydrate on the amount he is consuming. The 'general feeling' is that he is teething and this explains everything—loss of diet, the runs. And yet Penelope Leach says this is simply untrue.*[7]

A Family Care Clinic (FCC) nurse suggests that I have post-natal depression. As the Diaries reveal, I find the diagnosis almost laughable, and I still do. My point is a simple one—what is accomplished with the label 'post-natal depression'? Shouldn't we be trying to identify what is making the woman depressed? Shouldn't we ask—what in her experience of infant care depresses her? In my case, I knew exactly what was making me depressed.

Fri 14 May   Valerie (Family Care Clinic) thinks I have post-natal depression. I think it's natural to be depressed if your baby goes off his food for no apparent reason. Stephen's behaviour becomes odder and odder (more and more odd?). He awoke screaming for a bottle at 10 p.m. last night as I expected (having fed at 4 p.m). But would have stopped at 60 ml. or so. He clearly wanted more & with the distraction of a toy soldier he took 180 ml. & slept through to 5 a.m. I fear we have classic bottle

---

7   Penelope Leach (1988) *Baby & Child: From Birth to Age Five.* Second edition. London: Penguin Books.

2

rejection here & it is probably due to all my efforts (tricks) to get him to feed. Of course, this is a worry & of course I want a solution & help. The matter is more worrisome if, as it seems, he isn't keen on solids either. It could be that a combination of factors are operating (including teething?). I have to return to the Mothers' Hospital but will do so only for a day clinic to see if they can help. In the meantime I must relax. Stephen isn't going to starve or dehydrate on current consumption. I just need to find a way to see Stephen through this hiccough . . . Blew it, I'm afraid. I thought after his morning nap, he might like some solids. Tried his favourite, pumpkin. Let him taste it off my finger. Even that small amount made him gag and vomit . . . No one has yet resolved why Stephen begins to cry when he has had a few mouthfuls of solids. I'm tempted to turn to homeopathy but still tentative. I wish there were someone who could say where to go next . . . Fortunately I have no work pressures and enough money to cover contingencies. I remain curious to discover the cause of the problem. And more than this I remain perplexed & concerned that he seems to want the milk but can't seem to take it . . . What a strange world of uncertainty and contradiction I've entered.

Food Record: *Fri 14/5 4.45 a.m. (150 ml) with soldier . . . 7 a.m. (gagged on pumpkin & vomited).*

Diary: *Sat. 15 May/93 Stephen vomited back his bottle given at 5 a.m. this morning. I think he gagged on the phlegm in the throat from the cold. However, his reaction to the bottle is more dramatic than ever. In fact, he's displaying signs of classic colic. Took Stephen to the Doctor again who confirmed that his chest is clear & his throat only a little red. She suggested that childcare may not be the best place for him.*

Food Record: *Sat 15/5/93 12.30 a.m. Don't give Mylanta beforehand! Use toy to distract. 150 m. Must relax. He will come back for more if he wants it. 5.15 a.m. (keep teat tight to begin. 70 ml. Administer Mylanta. Head on pillow to one side. Squirt in SIDE). 120 ml. Had to be careful re gagging. 70 m. Vomited up half the bottle in bed.*

Food Record: *Sun 16/5/93 1.15 p.m.(100 ml. Using two baths)*

Diary: *Mon 17 May/93 The problem is that I've discovered that Stephen's feeding aversion is psychological, brought on by the trauma caused by choking on the phlegm in his throat. I know this because the decline in intake is related to the timing of the vomits. Also, I have been able to settle him down with warm baths to get something into him. Today then I'll have to be here for his feeds . . . I'm booked into a*

Mothers' Hospital day clinic. I wonder how they can help with this one.

Food Record: *Mon 17/5/93 5.45 a.m. (congested/Demazin/Multagen) 60 ml. with 2 baths. 1.30 pm. (190 ml. Really hungry. Then became upset and needed a bath to take extra 40 ml.) 9 p.m. Screaming. Would take 90 ml. only, half asleep on pillow. Difficult to settle. Panadol.*

Chapter 9

Hell Revisited

And so we arrive where we started. It's taken a while to get here but perhaps now you have a better understanding of both the complexity of the problem and of my state of mind. It is this combination which stands out as significant but no one addressed it. Instead there seemed to be a conviction that <u>either</u> Stephen, at five-and-a-half months old, had a physiological problem <u>or</u> a psychological problem (due to my reactions).

On Monday 17 May we attended a day clinic at the Mothers' Hospital. This is the event recorded in Chapter 1, the low point in my early days of mothering, the high point in the nightmare. I will always remember those words—'we have our ways', and watching the nurse 'force' food into Stephen's mouth. I will always remember the feeling of inadequacy produced in me. I will always remember being sent away more confused than when I arrived. On Friday 21 May, Stephen and I were back, this time for admission. Sometimes I slept in a room there; some nights I went back to our flat. Because I had more free time, my reflections on what was happening are more extensive than on other occasions.

Friday 21st May
Came in to the Mothers' Hospital yesterday morning. Stephen fed quite well for Esther, the sister on duty, but wouldn't feed for anyone else. At 8.30 p.m. they were discussing sedation. Fortunately, someone put a bottle in his mouth just as he awoke and he took it. (His total yesterday would have been 640 ml. Came in at 3.30 a.m. for a feed. They were trying again at 6.45 p.m.)

Saw Belinda, the skeptic [the one who said that Stephen was just stubborn; see Chapter 1] *who now admits that Stephen has* <u>something</u>—*a variant of reflux which requires treatment. She tells me, 'Your child has a feeding disorder'. I felt like saying something like, 'Well, what a surprise!' I replied, somewhat less sardonically, 'I told you that'.*

At the Monday day clinic (17 May), I had been given medication for reflux, some stuff which had to be given 15 minutes before a feed. I found the 15 minutes of screaming intolerable. Also, Stephen was so worked up by this time that he rejected the bottle. I also tried to put into practice the method of 'forced feeding' I had observed.

May 21/93 (continued). A few hours later. Collision with Dr Phelps. He found out (I wasn't hiding it) that I had gone to a chiropractor. I hadn't suspected that he was such a traditionalist. He was also upset that I wasn't *using the Cysapride [anti-reflux medicine]—now it seems I don't have to wait 15 minutes after administering it. Also—NB—yesterday Esther's feeding technique was explained in more detail & it is not <u>forced</u> feeding but <u>firm</u> feeding. Thank God I attempted to use it only once. I was certainly doing more damage than good. A little knowledge is indeed a dangerous thing.*

*Dr Phelps seems convinced that **I** am the problem— talked about the tense baby/tense mother syndrome. The nursing staff, even Belinda!, feels that Stephen's reflux is a problem. At least Dr Phelps is prepared to attempt to relieve this with a renewed barrage of medication. It seems the postural drainage may not be needed. Stephen's congestion seems to have improved & the cough is almost gone.*

How do I feel? A little under siege. People keep telling me I need to relax but Stephen's illnesses & bottle rejection have indeed made me tense. Dr Phelps says you offer the baby the bottle &, if he refuses, you give it a miss until later. He doesn't say how you live in the meantime— how/whether it is possible to go anywhere or take a baby anywhere when he is crying, screaming for a bottle, but unwilling to feed. He also doesn't explain why Stephen refuses to feed until he's starving. I don't see much help here. I will use the medications & hope they relieve the worst of the reflux symptoms. I will also go along with the non-traditionalists (the chiropractor and the kinesiologist). The latter at least has me as her target. [That is, she was willing to consider the pressures I was experiencing and how these 'fed' back into the problem.] *Since this is a critical part of the puzzle I must somehow believe in her enough to see if she can help. And I will go to talk to Valerie (Family Care Clinic). She also has me as the target & I am willing to see what she can do.*

+ a crucial questions remains—when Stephen is 'due' a bottle, makes hungry signals and then refuses the bottle, what do you do? Especially if you have just administered all the medication he's supposed to have. Do you give him a bath? (Dr Phelps says more that 2 a day is bad for his skin) Do you use distraction? firmness? or do you give it a miss? let him cry and try later? [had written 'let me cry'—how apt!] *What do you do if 'later' produces similar results? How often in this process do you pour the anti-reflux medicine into him?*

The Diaries describe a deep mistrust of the hospital staff. I want to know how this happened, and if it were avoidable. I can't help feeling that this us-versus-them scenario did not help Stephen.

21 May (continued) I feel compelled to watch Stephen constantly, keeping him asleep 'on the sly'—with a little patting, rocking—to prevent them from intervening, tucking him in on his side like he is in a straight-jacket, and letting him cry himself to sleep. I also feel as if I am under scrutiny. Last night it took me 30 minutes using 'my' techniques to get him to sleep. Today I was doing great & just as he had fallen asleep, Dr Phelps arrived. It then took a while (15 minutes) & rocking to resettle him. I now sit by his bedside, surreptitiously patting him when he stirs, trying to keep him asleep an 'acceptable' length of time. I sit like a 'watchman' protecting my infant son from trauma.

All the while I was acutely aware that my reactions were part of the problem. I engaged in a good deal of self-examination. My confusion and self-doubt are apparent, as is my rationalisation of what was happening.

21 May (continued) How do I learn to relax and return some balance to my life? I'm really puzzled and at a bit of a loss here. I know that some time away from Stephen is necessary & trusting him to others is also necessary. I know that I need to start getting out and taking care of myself. I know that to do all this I need to stop <u>caring</u> about Stephen's food intake and his crying. I have to say—'so he hasn't fed—so he'll get hungry—so he'll cry. I can do no more than offer him food.' With this, I will do all I can to guarantee that any distress he feels is alleviated. Can I use medication <u>and</u> touch healing? Can I try to strike a balance between traditional and non-traditional medicine?

Can I 'force' myself to relax? What an oxymoron that is! ... I need to find a mental state that allows me to function and indeed remain calm/happy through all this. Stephen generally seems to be a happy child—so I can't be doing it all wrong. He is content in company and plays by himself for reasonable lengths of time. There are certain things which upset him—having things pulled over his head, leaving the bath—but none of this is serious.

And feeding became a problem only after the viral throat infection, when I felt the responsibility of 'convincing' him to eat past the pain.

I'm now no longer sure that this is true. I think the problem goes further back to the failed breastfeeding and the screaming and sleepless nights this produced. The belief that my baby had screamed because he was hungry/starving induced a conviction in me that I would never allow this to happen again. The early Food Records also signal a preoccupation with Stephen's food intake some time before the viral pharangytis. Clearly, I wanted to believe that all our problems had a simple explanation. This made my behaviours *appear* rational, or at least explicable.

21 May (continued) Unfortunately, I seem to have continued to feel that this [helping Stephen 'feed past the pain'] *is my responsibility. Hence I have become obsessed with getting food into him. <u>This has got to stop!!</u> Stephen must be allowed to take what he wants when he wants it. My efforts are counterproductive. He, as a bright child, sees me as a 'food-enforcer'—<u>this has got to stop!!</u>*

Valerie says I need to analyse why I am so upset when Stephen takes a bad feed and so overjoyed when he takes a good feed. Partly, this is due to what I have just said/written. If he feeds, I feel that I have achieved my motherly responsibility. But I must admit/confess that in part it is due to the desire to restore some normalcy/ pattern to life. I was happy when Stephen ate predictably four-hourly. I could plan my life around that. Now I have to find a way to 'plan' a life around unpredictability. This is the greatest challenge I have faced and I have no option but to face it.

It's strange. I think back to a few weeks ago and I had become quite confident about feeding Stephen. I can't quite remember when it began to fall apart again. But I must also admit that at every feed there was a goal— getting Stephen to take a full feed so that I could then say that he wouldn't need food for four hours. To achieve this I always finished a feed on a tripillow. I suppose this remains acceptable so long as I stop persisting when Stephen indicates disinterest.

It's funny. I have had no difficulty implementing this approach with solids. I would never dream of forcing solids on Stephen. This is clearly because I have read that solids are incidental to his nutrition right now. Milk, I am told, is <u>absolutely crucial</u>. So, in all this, I feel I am responsible for Stephen's health and well-being. This is doubtless so, but I must cease looking at Stephen as a plant which needs watering or a pet which needs feeding. He is a person and, although he has no real sense of his own needs, he is beginning to assert his personality. And crucially he is telling me that he will <u>not</u> be forced to do things.

11.45 a.m. Stephen is currently in Belinda's arms facing a feed. She's one of the toughest in the business. I peeked & saw him crying—immediately felt distressed. It's five hours since his last feed & he was hungry. We carefully administered all the anti-reflux medicine. I suppose I hoped that that would be the end of it. I just heard him crying again. I suppose I need to recognise that either 1) the medication won't work; or 2) Stephen needs several painless feeding experiences to overcome his fear of feeding; or 3) Stephen may still be tense due to the past few days, though the nursing staff feel that 24 hours should be adequate for the 'tense mother' effect to wear off. It is quiet now & I pray he is feeding. I pray it doesn't hurt him. I pray he begins to find eating pleasurable again.

A few words about mothering. I'm in my room at the Mothers' Hospital. It's 8 p.m. I've had a glass of white wine and written a few letters. I tucked Stephen in about an hour ago in a quiet room. He was quite snuffly and his cough was back. I know he'll be due a feed shortly. I wish he were closer. I want to go and see how he's getting on. I want to protect him from noise and discomfort. I feel guilty that I'm so far away from him.

Re food, etc. I need to rethink my whole attitude to feeding Stephen. I've read somewhere that hunger is a part of child development, the partner of appetite. However, many of us associate it with pain & malnutrition. The message seems to be that the duty of the provider is to make the food available, not to guarantee that it is eaten. Now to apply it!

Sat. 22 May   The month marches on. I'm up nice & early—good, long sleep. Pop up to the nursery. Stephen had a difficult feed with Harriet at 8.30 p.m. last night. Took only 120 ml. Then slept well and took 200 ml. easily at 1.30 a.m. He has been asleep since. It is now 6.30 a.m. I am not surprised re the easy middle-night feed. He is always easier to feed when he's still drowsy. I wonder if any medication was used.

A thought as I sit waiting (7.30 a.m.) for Stephen to awake in the nursery. I have to stop thinking of Stephen as a being driven solely by his stomach. It is likely that my tendency to do this is due to 1) my feeling that his crying during the first six weeks of life was due to hunger—inadequate breast milk supply; 2) the fact that Stephen cries hysterically only when he wants to feed. I have managed to keep his other needs met. The child development literature tells me that by 3 to 6 months virtually all babies will wait for all meals & hunger does not produce significant prolonged screaming. Someone should tell Stephen!

1 p.m.   I cried an hour ago, in front of Belinda. Said I was depressed. She suggested leaving town for a week & leaving Stephen in her care. She suggested counselling for me and mentioned post-natal depression. Surely it's clear that I'm depressed because Stephen can't feed & sees eating as an ordeal. I wouldn't be depressed if he were OK.

And now we're going to try sedating Stephen for feeds for a few days. This too depresses me but I can't see any options right now.

2 p.m.   Stephen had his first feed sedated. Took 175 ml. without protest—about 10 minutes after 2.5 ml. Cloral(?) . . . I took some also. Pleased to say he is now playing happily—i.e. he is not completely doped! This is a transition measure and a desperation measure. We're hoping it will break the cycle and make feeding pleasurable again.

The good news is that at the 5.15 p.m. feed Stephen took 120 ml. & later finished the bottle lying in the playpen. The bad news is that they used distraction techniques. Surely one of the reasons I'm in here is because distraction works only for a time & that it's not a solution. There also seemed to be no clear policy on sedatives, regarding whether Stephen should have them for a number of feeds or 'if needed' and what 'if needed' means.

Sun 23 May   So—I wake up at 5.30 a.m. to check on my baby, and what do I find? They sedated him at 2.30 a.m. to get him to sleep through the night so that he would feed at convenient times for me. I'm furious but can't afford to show it. I have to remain diplomatic. So— there is a complete lack of clarity about what we are supposed to be doing for Stephen. The sister in charge said that, if yesterday Stephen hadn't been fed at 2.30 a.m, he probably would have fed well later. The assumption here is that his problem is hunger. No one seems to be hearing me and this is frustrating. It certainly confirms that I had better not fall apart. Stephen needs me.

The new sister coming on duty had the nerve to say that all that Stephen required was love & affection, & that she didn't think I was enjoying him. Jesus Christ! Are these people trying to make me depressed, to get a reaction out of me? She made me feel like shit, like a truly inadequate mother. You do begin to feel like a voice in the wilderness.

Harriet observed some of Stephen's strange eating habits last night. Why does a baby with reflux prefer to take his bottle lying flat on his back? Why does Stephen begin to take his solids (sitting up) and then begin to cry?

Note. Ruth says the dosage of Choral(?) . . . (2.5 ml.) is too strong to be used before every feed!!

6.45 p.m. I've now fed Stephen twice using the sedative. The first was completely successful. The second looked bad but came good. The difference was definitely the nurse. The first made me confident; the second made me feel like a bumbling idiot. But I overcame the problems. The key is definitely that Stephen needs to be happy and receptive to the feed. I'm not sure how this would work for an entire bottle—i.e. right now, with the Dormil [sedative], he is starting on a pillow in my arms. After he rebelled, I put him in the playpen. But you definitely need to give him time to settle down. Then later he took the cornflour custard & fruit really well.

They now tell me that I'll be woken for the night time feed. The only reason I object is because Stephen will be ravenous & hence very upset—especially given the time it takes to come and get me. Of course, this is true for all the breastfed babies as well. I must remember that he isn't really starving and that hunger pains are not lethal. Also, a little crying will make him sleep better afterwards.

Monday 24 May/93

I had been warned that I would be called for the night feed. Predictably, this did not happen. The message was not conveyed. Nonetheless, I woke every hour after 10 p.m. waiting for him.

Also, the message was transmitted that I didn't want Stephen fed if he woke c.10.30 p.m. How ridiculous! I didn't want him <u>woken</u> to feed him. Anyway, at least he didn't have a sedative to make him sleep.

The feed this morning went well. This was with Dormil.

Dr Phelps says Dormil is no longer being made. Suggested Panquil which contains a pain reliever which he says is useful for <u>these</u> babies—an admission re the significance of reflux in Stephen's case.

25 May/93

6 a.m. Yesterday Stephen did very well, taking 950 ml. (most of it without sedative) & some solids, though he still wasn't keen. Re the solids, since using the new anti-reflux medication (Zantac), Stephen doesn't cry after a few mouthfuls of solids . . . Last night Stephen took 130 ml. at 2 a.m.—not really interested. Nurses seem to feel that he should be able to drop this feed. I'd be happy for him to do so but, as I explained, I've been so concerned with getting him to feed that <u>when</u> seemed to be the least of my worries.

It is important to see how Stephen's feeding problems and sleeping problems were interconnected. I was being encouraged to 'manage' his sleeping problems by cutting feeds, but I still felt that feeding was the priority. I even woke him for feeds on occasion. Here, one of my concerns was that Stephen had to be relaxed to feed. Hence, I couldn't just wait for him to demand food because he would then be too agitated to take it. My best chance of getting him to feed was when he was sleepy, that is, just coming out of a sleep. This led eventually to my technique of 'rocking him off' to sleep before a feed. (This is the technique of swivelling my body described at the beginning of Chapter 8). All of these interventions produced huge instabilities in Stephen's sleeping patterns.

Often the Diaries talk about 'moving on', even about the nightmare 'being over'. They talk about the need to recognise when problems are 'new', not a recurrence of 'the nightmare'. These entries indicate attempts on my behalf to find a kind of resolution, to suggest to myself that things were going to improve. In fact, they didn't improve for months. The entries also indicate a growing tendency to sheet home responsibility for the problem/s to myself. It is difficult to say what caused this. It was certainly an interpretation of events others encouraged me to hold.

25 May /93 (continued)
The nightmare may be over—I was going to write 'is over', in my new optimistic frame of mind, but there is still a slight tensing in the pit of my stomach when I face feeding Stephen. Here is where I have some work to do and quickly. The realisation that hunger pains cannot be that excruciating & that older babies should be able to wait—in fact that appetite is a good thing—may help. On the other side, the realisation that Stephen needs to be relaxed and rested for a feed and that I should anticipate his hunger puts me under pressure to create the right circumstances for him to feed. Even last night, while I was feeding him, he twisted his head to follow the nurse in the room . . . I must also get over my fear that he will gag on solids & vomit back the bottle. My fear here is that it will lead to another spate of food rejection. But, as Dr Phelps said, some babies vomit all the time & it doesn't put them off food. It was probably just a coincidence that Stephen rejected food following the vomit incident.

I can remember the day we left the Mothers' Hospital. I had mixed feelings. I was pleased to be escaping the scrutiny and judgment, and I was pleased to have Stephen under my control again—so that they couldn't make him cry any more. But I was also afraid. The only times Stephen had fed well, he had been sedated. Now they told me that there was nothing more they could do for me/us— other than to provide prescriptions for a whole swathe of medications. I was told that it was 'over to me'. I wanted to ask how sedation was a solution. I wanted someone to tell me how to cope. No one gave me this information. Hence, it is not surprising that our problems did not go away. I continued to find ways to 'manage'; some of them helped, some of them made things worse.

Chapter 10

Madness?

One of the truisms to emerge from my experience of mothering is that things never stay the same. Mothers talk about 'breakthroughs', some trivial, some significant. Crawling and walking are among the latter, being able to replace the dummy themselves one of the former. And, of course, there are new illnesses and new physiological developments, including teething. Since both of these affected feeding, they involved a degree of trauma for Stephen and me that is probably unusual in other situations. The cycle of Stephen's physiological distress over feeding and my psychological fear of food rejection meant that we were a long way from resolution of our difficulties.

I believe, in fact, that my problems became very much worse. I watched myself become erratic, depressed, unstable. This really frightened me. After all, I was an academic. I was rational, in control. From a distance, it is fascinating to observe how close to the edge of insanity I trod. Perhaps part of the lesson here is that we are all much closer to the edge than we realise. I certainly no longer take my state of mind for granted. Nor do I find instability in myself or in others unexpected.

The Food Records for this period indicate a continuing preoccupation—now, I would say obsession—

with the amount Stephen consumed and the struggle to find a routine which would make my life a little more predictable. Each recorded feed now includes references to the medication I administered. Stephen's bowels also continue to be monitored. The daily tally of total consumption of milk appears in each entry. Below is a complete record of our first day home from the Mothers' Hospital. Excerpts from the Food Records are then interspersed with sections from the Diaries. Stephen was now almost six months old.

Food Record: Thurs. 27/5/93.
1. *5.45 a.m. (190 ml.) Cysapride + Zantac + Multagen. Small firm b/o. + 8 a.m. pears*
2. *9.45 a.m. (120 ml) not hungry (? re pears) + Cys +Zan*
3. *1.40 p.m.(180 ml.) small b/o. Another b/o. Cys +Zan. (sub-total 490 ml.) + pumpkin*
4. *5.45 p.m.(190) + custard. Pebble.*
5. *11.30 p.m.(200 ml.).*
Total [circled]: 880 ml.

Diary: *Fri. 28 May.   Stephen has really settled down. We haven't had any real traumas with feeding. I just have to remember that, when he pulls his head away, it's usually wind. He's an easy baby in many ways, tolerant and good-natured. I love to hear him laugh. Putting him* to sleep is also easy so long as 'rocking off' is used. This can only be for a time.

Sat 29 May
Stephen has developed a bacterial infection on top of a virus. So he's now coughing constantly and is off his food—again! I need to be careful not to judge his current rejection of food as a recurrence of the 'nightmare'. I need to loosen up. For the first time today felt I might be succumbing (terrible spelling), giving in to post-natal depression. I had some difficulty making decisions & said silly things when Stephen wouldn't eat . . . I wish I could find the right person to help out. More than this, I wish Stephen would get well for a while. And even more than this, I really need to stop worrying and to get on with life and with life with Stephen . . . I see the pile of letters et al. on my desk which require replies. All this seems so distant, as do friends, and the idea of a dinner out, or a movie. I really must find a way to get closer to normalcy—for my sake & for Stephen's.

Food Record: *Sat 29/5/93 5 p.m. Septrin. Total for day: 610 ml.*

Diary: *Sun. 30 May. Stephen slept really well last night & is obviously improved health-wise today. We had a lovely play together. He has a happy disposition & is great fun to be with . . . He has been difficult to settle for naps. I think this is due to the congestion & coughing. I* *finally succeeded in settling him on his side. I now wait for him to wake for a feed. He took only 100 ml. at 7 a.m. but had fed well (170 ml.) at 3 a.m. I expect him to be hungry now but must accept what he takes. I keep reminding myself that any refusal to eat now is not the same problem. I have to keep remembering what it <u>was</u> like. He actually used to scream when first set on the tripillow. Now, on the pillow in my arms, he starts drinking well usually. He sometimes becomes agitated and pulls his head away. But he keeps coming back until something is troubling him. Then he cries. This could be wind but it could also be reflux, despite the medication. I usually then lie him on his back on the ground. He often takes more but sometimes gets confused & bats the bottle away with his hands. I have to devise techniques— holding one arm quiet by treading on the sleeve of his jumper & keeping the other hand occupied with a toy. Found a way this p.m. to minimise gagging—holding the bottle to one side. He did unfortunately gag & vomit on solids.*

Food Record: *Sun 30/5. 10 p.m. I woke him. Hope I don't regret this. 170 ml.*

Diary: *Mon 31/5 The feeds are still tricky. This morning he pulled away quickly but took a decent amount on his back. At 1 p.m. he seemed to be feeding against a resistance. I think it must have been wind since a little later he took the rest easily. I really must slow down his feeds and take time to wind him . . . Dr Phelps's offices today said he wanted me to go ahead with tests in Sydney, ph probe and endoscopy. I said I didn't intend to if Stephen is feeding well.*

Food Record: *Mon. 31/5. 5 p.m. They* [the Mothers' Hospital staff] *said not all feeds would be as successful. This was reminiscent of the old terror, except if I stay calm I can get him to take most but not all. Finished bottle after huge burp!*

Food Record: *Tues. 1/6/93 10 a.m. Thought we were facing disaster. Rejected on pillow and on floor. Rocked him off a little to settle him. Then pinned him on floor, took out dummy and put in bottle immediately. Took 150 ml. Then break. Waited 10 minutes till burp. Finished bottle dangling key. Given weight gain, I'll let him sleep through tonight.*

Diary: *Wed. 2 June. Stephen is half a year old today & I'm very lucky. He is almost always in a good mood & loves to smile. I've enjoyed the last few days with him . . . Sometimes it's hard to get up in the morning, especially if I've been monitoring his movements all night, ready to respond the moment he seems hungry. I actually ended up waking him at 2 a.m., simply so I could get some sleep. Then as usual he surfaced at 5 a.m. I didn't think he'd be hungry by 6 a.m. but something was troubling him. I tried offering him the bottle in bed & he turned his head away. I took my time & with repeated offers over the next 45 minutes he took almost the whole bottle. But I don't think he was very hungry. Difficult to tell when rejection is due to lack of hunger or to some internal disturbance (reflux?).*

Thurs 3 June/93   I continue to use the technique of rocking him to sleep in my arms before a feed. A great success, but I don't think it is an answer.

Fri. 4 June.   Hell of a night! Stephen went to bed early & then couldn't get back to sleep at 1.30 a.m. I felt quite stressed which didn't help . . . Part of the problem may be due to my intervention/manipulation to get him to eat. I'm worried because he seems to want only 4 bottles—under 800 ml. And of course he's not taking solids now either, due to his congestion + antibiotics.

It seems to me *post hoc* that there is an expectation that mothers can instinctively read their baby's signals—when they are hungry, when they are tired, when they need something, when they don't. In fact, I have on occasion fallen back on this folk wisdom myself. We will see later that I cut back on the medication because I was certain that it was having no effect. At the same time, however, the Diaries and Food Records tell a sad tale about just how difficult it is to interpret signals. It is possible that this problem escalated for me because I had concluded that reading signals properly was crucial to our success at feeding. That is, I knew that if I waited too long to feed Stephen, he would become too agitated to feed. The same was true if he were tired. It is equally possible, however, that there is no instinct which automatically translates infant screams into clear instructions.

Sat 5 June/93 Dr Hammond has put us back on demand feeding. This means I don't need to wake him for feeds! . . . I remain concerned about rejection & how to get the medication into him prior to a feed.

Sun 6 June/93 Today I've used the 'rocking off' technique before feeds & it's been a complete success. I know Dr Hammond wanted me to start feeding on demand. Part of the problem is that I'm not sure of Stephen's hunger signals. They are very like his tired signals, and mixing them up is a disaster. This becomes more likely if he goes more than 4 hours between feeds, unless I can manage to guarantee a good sleep in the run up to a feed. This of course is easy if I rock him off in my arms. So it accomplishes several goals—guarantees he's rested, simplifies the interpretation of signals & keeps him relaxed. I know I will have to abandon it one day.

Chapter 11

What's the Problem?

On Monday 7 June,= 1993 Stephen, now six-and-a-half months old, and I flew to Sydney. Some friends, Terri, David and their four-year-old daughter, Hannah, invited us to stay for a few weeks. They had visited us in the Mothers' Hospital and could see that we needed help. I will always be grateful for their generosity. There were also some well-known clinics in Sydney we needed to visit. And Dr Phelps had lined up some tests for Stephen. I also saw a psychologist for the first time. The Diaries and Food Records contain reflections on my continuing desire to understand the problem, reflections which fluctuate between self-blame and cautious comments on larger structural problems.

Wednesday 9 June/93   Not doing too bad considering. There have been a few adjustment problems—figuring out how to a get a bottle to Stephen quickly enough up several flights of stairs [my friends lived in a three-storey terrace house]. *Also when I try to settle him, subsequent resettlings mean standing by upstairs or mounting the stairs quickly. The good things are numerous. Stephen seems to be enjoying himself & he is sleeping well at night (which is great since I'm in the same room). However, he is taking only 4 bottles a day (around 800 ml.) & shows no interest in solids . . . I've been 'managing' feeds by generally ensuring that Stephen is sleepy* [and hence relaxed] *before each feed (allowing 4 and a half hours between feeds to ensure he's hungry). Inadvertently I had cut back on the medication . . . He rejects the bottle after about 120 ml. but takes the rest quite happily on his back on the floor—very unreflux-like behaviour!*

Food Record: *Fri 11/6   Had reduced Zantac to 2x4 ml. to 1x4 ml. to naught. Had reduced Cysapride to day feeds (3x1.5 ml.) to 1x1.5 ml. to naught. Today, prune juice and Multagen for constipation.*

Terri arranged for a baby sitter to take care of Stephen so she and I could go out. It was the first real break I had had since his birth.

9 June/93 (continued)   I feel much better after 2 hours to myself & knowing Stephen is being kindly cared for. I clearly need a little distance from him to gain perspective. I need to make sure that somehow I cease being so obsessive about his well being. As Terri says, babies cry & I need to allow him to express his 'bad' feelings. I mustn't repress him. I must allow him to be Stephen rather than 'the baby'. By this I mean I have to start thinking of Stephen as a whole person not just as a bundle of needs. It's amazing he's as good natured as he is given my state of mind about the whole experience.

Sat 12 June/93   I'm sitting in Terri and David's upstairs bedroom enforcing controlled crying on Stephen for his 10.15 a.m. nap. I've discovered that I'm very lucky that his sleep patterns are in no worse state than they are. That is, he seems to sleep well at night & to be able to resettle himself. Last night slept from 6 p.m. to 5 a.m!! But his day-time sleeps are & always have been another matter, to the extent that I started rocking him off in my arms and doing so again when he stirred after half-an-hour. Things had deteriorated recently, due to another cold, to me having to hold him [for the whole nap]. *Today I'm trying two new approaches: 1) putting him down for a nap after a feed instead of playing first; & 2) swaddling him in a sheet to prevent him from removing the dummy.*

New sleep patterns are not the only breakthrough. I seem to be able to feed Stephen without trauma, albeit using unconventional techniques. He takes the bottle lying on his back with me squatting/standing over him. I have to pin his left arm with my foot & keep the other hand occupied with a toy. Weird, but it works. Terri can also feed him this way & Mary [the baby sitter] *(mother of 13!) developed her own technique—lying him flat in a pram. What is significant here is that other people besides myself can feed Stephen.*

Further developments. Had my pre-admission interview at the Mothers' Hospital here. The sister Patricia agreed that Stephen did not look like a reflux baby—encouraged me to follow my inclination & take him off medication. I had been cutting back on the Zantac & Cysapride already. Today I won't give Stephen any. There are no signs of indigestion post-feed & when he insists on a break midway in the bottle, it seems to be either for a rest or a burp.

The other breakthroughs are on the personal level. I am finally feeling more relaxed about Stephen's feeds. Of course, it is possible that this is because they are going so well. But I would like to think that I am finally loosening up about the notion of 'getting food into him'. I realise that it is crucial that the breakthrough be at this level in order to make it meaningful & to prevent food arising as an issue between Stephen & myself at a later stage.

Here Christine from a support service aiming at 'early intervention' deserves some credit. This was my first go at counselling & I was impressed with how connections were made where I hadn't expected them. These were: 1) I spoke about how the children in my family had to praise my Mum's cooking constantly to make her feel worthwhile & to keep her in a good mood. The connection between food & mothering then was fraught in my background. Christine more or less cautioned that I didn't want to recreate a pattern where Stephen was held responsible for my moods, be it by his eating or otherwise . . . I also confessed that I decided to have Stephen because of a certain emptiness in my life. Again, there is a danger here that, like my Mum, I could begin to

live through him and hence to load him with respon-
sibility for my happiness. Though I never thought it
would be necessary to say this—I need to keep my other
interests (research, sport, etc.) to prevent this from
happening. I must not become obsessed with Stephen!
2) I mentioned to Christine that I was disturbed by the
way Stephen's feeds affected my moods. A good feed left
me euphoric, a bad feed, depressed. She probed my
attitudes to eating/weight re myself and I suddenly
remembered how, pre-Stephen, I used to become
overjoyed if I dropped a few pounds at my daily weigh-in
& profoundly depressed if the scales indicated a gain. I
also remember acknowledging to myself at the time that
these reactions were over the top. The connection then is
obvious. I have transferred my concern/self esteem from
my own appearance to Stephen. As in point one, I am
threatening to live through him. In an attempt to bring
this to a halt, I am going to start taking more interest in
my appearance. Had all my hair cut off yesterday. It's
now pert and easy care.

My friend Terri had not found motherhood easy
either. She therefore was sympathetic to my plight.
Being further along (her daughter was now four
years old), she had had the time to reflect on the
kinds of difficulties she faced and the reasons for
them. Given my feminist background, I was
interested in her ideas. Until this point in time, I had

been in survival mode and had had little energy to commit to theorising my dilemmas. I now began to consider these issues, if only at a superficial level.

Sat. 12 June /93 (continued) Terri has some interesting ideas for a book on professional women and motherhood—trying to explain why she & I (& others) have found it so difficult to come to terms with a baby. One point she stressed the other day was that it had been possible, given the way our society is organised, for both of us to go through a great deal of our lives without having anything to do with babies or children. So we entered this 'other world' completely unprepared. There are levels here which need exploring. Do we (professional women) cope worse? Or is motherhood equally demanding for all women, but we (i.e. professional women) are more prepared to protest or have more opportunities to protest?

Tues 15 June/93   I'd have to say that things are going really well. Stephen is eating again, and seems to be keen on solids. I find it strange, however, how easily I become concerned about things—i.e. Stephen's behaviour has been a little odd—hyper, lots of experimenting with screaming, volatile—and yet I'm sure he's well rested. This could be one of those periods of frustration before a growth in development. He also has a raw patch on his bottom lip & I start worrying about a recurrence of viral pharangytis.

Wed 16 June/93   How can things look so grim on some days, so great on others? Yesterday, I was convinced that Stephen had reached the age where he could keep himself awake. Hence I resorted to controlled crying yesterday and this morning. What an ordeal! And after speaking to a range of experts I discovered there is no set approach to settling babies and Stephen may need special attention given his recent illness.

Occasionally the Diaries make it crystal clear how puzzled I was, how desperately I wanted things to settle into a pattern. This is a recurrent theme which needs explaining. I have a stab at this in several places. Another recurring theme is the linking of sleeping and feeding problems. That is, my concerns about getting Stephen to eat meant that I was willing to disrupt his sleep. More and more, however, I began trying to plan his feeds to see if I could guarantee *myself* a decent sleep. The tensions between these two goals get played out over this period.

Thurs 17 June/93   Stephen [six-and-a-half months old] woke for a 1.30 a.m. bottle but otherwise slept well. He was also hungry for breakfast at 7.30. He is now asleep. Slept 9.30 a.m. to 10.30 a.m.+. This is clearly not after his feed but it was when he was tired. Now I expect that he'll eat around 11 a.m., sleep from 1p.m. to 3 p.m., feed at 3 p.m. The tricky bit is his next nap which must not become the long sleep. That is, he must wake around 5 p.m. or so and feed around 7 p.m. Then we have a good chance of his sleeping through [the night]. *We'll get this right eventually.*

Fri 18 June/93   Rough night last night & just when I'd 'planned' for Stephen to sleep through. Had his last bottle close to 7 p.m. Woke for the first time at 11.30 p.m. I was convinced he couldn't be hungry & resettled him. Called again at 12.30 & took some juice. Another call at 1.30 a.m. At 2 a.m. I gave in & fed him. He took 180 ml. He seemed to be warm at the earlier waking (first night in the so-called tea-tree snuggle bed) so I removed the sleeping bag . . . Woke again at 4.20 a.m. so I took him into bed with me where he slept quite well till 6 am . . . Noted the appearance of the dreaded patches of thrush. Also, a small blister on the top of his mouth. I pray it isn't a recurrence of viral pharangytis. Just couldn't go through that ordeal again. Must get him to a doctor this a.m.

Mon. 21 June/93   Lovely weekend. Stephen is a delight when he's awake. He doesn't seem to need long sleeps all the time. Unfortunately, the nights haven't been all that successful. For the last 4 nights Stephen has been waking every two hours. I keep trying to figure out the problem. I keep experimenting with bedding. Last night I made sure he wasn't hungry but he still took a bottle just after midnight. Maybe he didn't need it but I'm never sure.

Nor am I sure how to deal with the night wakings. The whole issue is complicated by the fact that we're sleeping in the same room. I react too quickly . . . There seems to be some feeling that it's teeth. I don't really think so. The pattern of waking is so regular. It's like the normal sleep pattern except he is having trouble resettling.

Food/Sleep Record: *Mon 21/6   Bedded 6.45 p.m. Woke 8 p.m., 9p.m., 9.20 p.m.(Panadol), 11 p.m., 1.15 p.m. (unswaddled him), 4.15 a.m. (bottle!!)*

Diary: *Thurs. 24 June/93   Quick entry. Still problems with sleep though pattern erratic. Last night slept well till 1.15 a.m., then couldn't resettle. Seemed congested. I'll make sure the vaporiser is on all night tonight . . . Second meeting with Christine ('early intervention' counsellor). She is lining me up with a psychologist in Canberra & a pediatric physiologist for Stephen (some concern re his motor skills development). I'm beginning to see the practice of the theory that professionals are very good at making work for each other!*

She also suggested massage as a way of creating 'trust' between Stephen & me, and kept talking about his need for reassurance. There are some heavy insinuations in this advice. I think that Stephen & I relate great! He sleeps in my arms readily, after a few minutes, and trusts me to feed him. I think his (& my) problems are few & there is little need for intervention, early or otherwise.

Finally she suggested that Stephen's recent night wakings are due to my attempt a few days ago to use controlled crying. That is truly bizarre. Stephen cried for no more than a total of 10 minutes. Any baby can cry that long without suffering emotional trauma. I think we have a combination of factors waking Stephen—primarily his nasal congestion & consequent dry throat (tonight I'll bring up some boiled water & a little prune juice & see how that goes). It seems he's producing pebbles again.

In all this analysis, where is Stephen the person? I'm so tired of looking at him as a combination of functions— eating, sleeping, etc. I am really beginning to enjoy his company and I know that this will increase with time. I actually like the little guy & his sunny disposition. His smiles continue to light up my day.

Where in all this is my paid labour? It will return to importance & soon. I really do want to do this book with Terri. I think it's important, vital. The one on affirmative action will also bear traces of my recent experiences. There will certainly be more focus on the way the domestic scene is either excluded from consideration, or included as a way of reducing its significance—i.e. it is only to do with women.

Many people, particularly students, are curious to know if my experience of mothering changed my feminism in any way. I tell them that I believe that my work has always been child friendly. *Same Difference* (Allen & Unwin, 1990), for example, insisted on the need for childrearing to be acknowledged as an important social activity. I tell them, however, that now I would write about these issues with more passion!

There are other differences. I used to think that childcare was a clear and obvious option for working mothers. I used to see it as a panacea for everyone. I have learnt that there are situations where childcare cannot work. Sick children and some sensitive children will need a different kind of environment.

I also used to think that mothering was a relatively easy thing to do. Hence, I believed that combining it with paid labour would be a cinch. I can remember thinking that it should be possible to write while taking care of an infant. This may be true for some. It certainly wasn't true for me.

I do not think that feminism ever denigrated motherhood. I would not agree with those critics who insist that feminists think that the key to self-esteem lies in paid work. But I do think that feminists bring their personal experiences to their analyses. Those who felt trapped by motherhood may well produce studies which convey the impression that mothering is a negative and limiting experience. The point here is that it is indeed easy to feel trapped by motherhood in a society as unresponsive as ours to the challenges of mothering. Hence, it shouldn't be surprising if some feminist analyses convey this impression. My experience, therefore, emphasised for me the need for greater social sensitivity to the isolation, sleep-deprivation, and traumas which constitute motherhood for so many women.

Sat. 26 June/93   Another unsettled night. Stephen went to bed at 7 p.m. after a bottle. Needed resettling again at 8 p.m., again at midnight & 2 a.m. Took a bottle at 5 a.m. & couldn't resettle. I awoke (i.e. got up), tired & fragile. I then probably came in too early with the 8.30 a.m. feed. Stephen definitely has less appetite, even for solids. His stool is firm & seems to require effort. The pumpkin is coming through almost undigested. His system must be working overtime. The good news is that he seems less inclined to 'go over the top', either when he's hungry or tired. This could be because I'm reading his signals better & getting in early. It could also mean that he is graduating from infancy. He definitely replaced his own dummy this morning & seemed very pleased with himself.

Sun 27 June/93.   Stephen slept better last night & consequently so did I. Difficult to say why. Difficult even to remember all the variables. Surely it was coincidence that it was bath day. Must keep track of this. Can't ignore the fact that I gave him 1 ml. Panadol at 7.30 p.m. because he was warm (there certainly is teething going on). His wakings, other than early in the evening, occurred at 2.30 a.m. & 4.20 a.m. On both occasions I was able to resettle him by giving him the dummy & putting him on his side . . . We're still looking for a schedule. I don't like the one he was on yesterday which started with a bottle at 5 a.m., breakfast at 8.30, lunch at 12, bottle at 3.30 p.m., solids at 5 p.m. & waiting/keeping him up till 7 p.m. for a final bottle which he was too tired to take. Today we're back on the 6/10/2/6 regime . . . I'll hold off on the solids till around 6 or 6.30 p.m. Then he might get through the night. Yesterday he had 5 bottles (850 ml.). Four bottles should suffice.

Food Record: *Sun 27/6 9.30 a.m. Blew it. Thought he was hungry. Took only 120 ml. Could be tired of milk. 5.30 p.m.(rejection!! should I stop the feed and offer solids? Should I try solids first?)*

Diary: *Mon 28 June /93 Stephen slept well last night but I'm afraid it was due to the Panadol. When he called me four times before 9 pm, I gave him a dose & when he seemed unable to settle at 12.30, I did the same. Don't know if his teeth are troubling him or not. Can't keep using Panadol as a sedative.*

More serious. He rejected the bottle twice yesterday & it seemed a return to the old nightmare. I must try to identify the differences, if there are any. He doesn't reject the bottle outright though he seems inclined to. He cuts out half way & won't be tempted back. Has he now seen through the new range of tricks? or are his teeth the problem? or is he trying to say he prefers solids?

There is a crucial difference, of course. He is not crying and rejecting solids. He seems keen on them. Today, when (if) he rejects the bottle, I must not persist too long, for fear of recreating the degree of rejection we had before. Instead, I'll stop, take a break (15 minutes or so), and offer him solids. Mary [the baby sitter and mother of thirteen] *has been suggesting this all along.*

Again, I try to pin down the reasons for my fear of [bottle] *rejection. I think it's mainly that then (if he does not take a full feed), I will not know when he's hungry again. That is, I will have to read his signals & I'm not very good at this. Or, I will misread his signals, giving him a bottle when he isn't ready, exacerbating the problem. Or waiting too long and then, because he is agitated, he'll also rebel.*

Wed. 30 June. Another bad night. Used Panadol. Didn't help much. Can't seem to figure out what makes a good night or a bad one.

Occasionally, in the Diaries, I reflect upon how mothering changed me as a person. I believe that I have changed in many ways. I also believe that it is unclear if these changes are for the good or not.

Wed. 30 June (continued) Collision with Terri yesterday. She didn't feel I was giving enough. I know it's true that everyone else takes a distant second place in my thoughts & feelings to Stephen. I hadn't realised I was ignoring her. Not quite sure what is expected of me. I ask about her plans/feelings, etc. as often as I can. I try to help by entertaining Hannah. Not sure what else is expected. Perhaps it's as with my other friends. Terri expected me to be the way I was before and to fill the role I used to fill, of mentor, of listener. Unfortunately, I don't seem to have the energy to fill that role right now.

It is difficult to explain or to rationalise to someone who is not a mother just how one's child becomes a full-time preoccupation. Whatever else you are doing, a part of you is with them. Whatever else you are doing, you are simultaneously planning things for them. These could be necessary things, like picking them up from childcare, or fun things, like fitting in a trip to the park. This preoccupation may put pressures on friendships, particularly pre-motherhood friendships. It also means that the obligations of paid labour are put into perspective. None of this means that mothers make less efficient workers. Rather, the ability to balance these many dimensions of human functioning is a testament to their capacity to handle complexity.

Chapter 12

Fitting In

Between 2 and 9 July, my friends, Stephen, now seven months old, and I had an indulgent holiday in Coolum, Queensland. I started a new journal at that time, where I attempted to reflect more critically on my situation. The fact that I was able to do this is a sign that I was rested enough to think straight. It was also therefore a sign that Stephen and I were moving on, though we still had a long way to go. In this journal, which also covers our return to Canberra, there are fewer and fewer entries, indicating that things were settling down and that my energy was being diverted more and more to paid labour.

The nature of the problem seems to have changed from feeding to sleeps. This is indicated in the Food Records which now tended to be rather straight-forward but to have supplementary notes on how often and when Stephen woke up during the night. I may never know why food became less of an issue. It was probably because Stephen was eating more and more solids, which no longer upset him. This in turn could have been because he no longer experienced heartburn. Feeding remained tricky, however. This was mainly because of the technique I had developed to get Stephen to take a bottle. There are few places where you can lie a child on his back, pin his arm and dangle a toy to give him a bottle, without interruption. I was also still almost the only person who could successfully give him a bottle. So, for as long as milk remained a key part of his diet, feeds would remain a shaping event in our lives. It is, of course, possible that Stephen could now have resumed a more normal bottle-feeding posture, but I was afraid to try it. There seems no doubt that, by this time in the story, how Stephen fed or did not feed had more to do with my fears than his needs.

July 2 Friday 1993 Early. Stephen woke at 4 a.m. (after waking at 10 p.m. and 1 a.m.) for a bottle. I didn't mind feeding him as I made rapid calculations and deduced we could get almost all the way to our destination (Coolum) without another bottle (I plan to offer him one at 8 a.m.) . . . It's a shame our lives continue to be dominated by feeds but I sense that things are changing. Stephen looked up at me quite calmly as he fed this morning. He was lying in my arms on a pillow. The Mothers' Hospital nurse who interviewed me in Sydney would almost have approved. I will do everything in my power not to turn Stephen over to them. They explained that, if I wanted help with his sleep pattern, I had to take the whole package & that included that Stephen would feed in my arms whether he liked it or not. I can't quite understand this philosophy. Why this commitment to orthodoxy?

It's the same with meal times. My goal is supposed to be to get Stephen to eat 3 meals a day, when 'we' do. The fact that many nutritionists think we'd all fare better health-wise with more frequent, smaller feeds is ignored. The determination is to force conformity to existing regimes—and so the system is perpetuated. I'm not being melodramatic. Our system (Western, industrial, capitalist) is run by the clock. Early child-rearing seems aimed at implanting that clock in each newborn.

Of course, most of this implanting is unconscious as we who are mothers with paid work struggle to make our child/children fit into the schedule demanded by work commitments. This indeed seems to have been a major driving element in this narrative. From the outset I sought a pattern. I wanted Stephen's needs and feeds to become predictable so that I could slot him into a routine. His feeding disorder made this extremely difficult. But I don't think that our experience is totally idiosyncratic. In fact, I believe that our lives, Stephen's and mine, are simply a more dramatic illustration of the challenges and pressures facing many, if not most, parents. I should add that Stephen is, at the time of writing, eight years old, and he knows how to tell the time. He continues to be a 'snacker', but in general we now 'fit in'—our mealtimes conform to a routine determined by work and school hours.

Sunday afternoon. 5th July/93   There has been little time to write or read. It's delightful here [Coolum] *and I'm enjoying myself, swimming, eating well and spending lovely times with Stephen. He enjoys travelling in the backpack. He's been giving the baby sitter hell, some of it my fault. But there is an amusing side. This very experienced grandmother has had to resort to taking Stephen on the shuttle to settle him. Seems he breaks into grins the moment they climb on board.*

Tues 6 July.   Great visit with brother Don and his family. Got to meet my new niece, Shannon Lee. She is what they call a 'good baby'. She eats & sleeps. Stephen has been a delight, though his night sleeps are a disaster.

I was surprised to find that there is an incident missing from the journal account for Coolum. I was surprised because I remember it so clearly. Perhaps I was too embarrassed to record it. Perhaps I couldn't quite put on paper the clear evidence that my state of mind was fragile, that I had a residual problem from Stephen's feeding history.

What happened? One day, as I was giving Stephen a bottle in a quiet room, Terri's young daughter, Hannah, walked in. Of course, this meant that Stephen was distracted and stopped feeding immediately. He had just begun a bottle. I snapped at her, told her to get out. She ran out in tears. Now, it is clear that Stephen was not going to starve if he missed this bottle. He was not going to be malnourished. And he probably wouldn't scream with hunger. My reaction was uncalled for. My reaction was irrational. This was not the only time something like this happened. It scared me and led me to pursue a psychologist on my eventual return to Canberra.

Fri 9 July. The week [in Coolum] *flew by. Got a little reading done but find I'm more interested in things like* The Secret of Happy Children *by Steve Biddulph than Meryle Kaplan's* Mothers' Images of Motherhood.[8] *The latter actually makes an argument similar to mine in* Same Difference. *She suggests that those feminists who focused on women's 'difference' (e.g. Gilligan, Chodorow),[9] on women's supposed caring natures, were engaged in wishful thinking, disillusioned as they were with our uncaring society. She argues that women's feelings are*

---

8   Steve Biddulph (1988) *The Secret of Happy Children.* Sydney: Bay Books. Meryle Mahrer Kaplan (1992) *Mothers' Images of Motherhood: Case Studies of Twelve Mothers.* London: Routledge.

9   Carol Bacchi (1990) *Same Difference: Feminism and Sexual Difference.* Sydney: Allen & Unwin; Carol Gilligan (1982) *In a Different Voice: Psychological Theory and Women's Development.* Cambridge: Harvard University Press; Nancy Chodorow (1978) *The Reproduction of Mothering: Psychoanalysis and the Sociology of Gender.* Berkeley: University of California Press.

more complex/contradictory than this. Biddulph emphasises assertive, positive parenting. He offers guidelines on dealing with tantrums.

My preference for Biddulph at this time reveals simply the need for day to day assistance with childrearing. I find his books on raising boys, with all the stuff on male role models, appalling![10] The point Kaplan makes is a very important one. She is showing how those feminists who 'go soft' on mothering, who talk about a maternal voice or a maternal ethic, in an attempt to (over)compensate for feminism's supposedly negative take on mothering, really paint mothers into a corner. They put forward another version of idealised mother-hood which mothers then try to live up to. From my position today I'd suggest that any idealised version of motherhood makes mothering more difficult. Rather, I believe that we need more detailed descriptions of the messy reality of mothering and the forces which contribute to this—inflexible work schedules, medical orthodoxy and assumptions that mothering is natural and hence easy. This belief is the reason I have gone public with my and my son's highly personal drama.

---

10 Steve Biddulph (1994) *Manhood*. Sydney: Finch Press; *Raising Boys: Why boys are different and how to help them become happy and well-balanced men*. Sydney: Finch Press.

Chapter 13

Moving On

Back in Canberra (Stephen was now seven-and-a-half months old), I began making moves to return to (paid) work. This was becoming necessary as my long-service leave was running out.

Friday 16 July/93   Home almost a week from Sydney (& Coolum) which both seem far away. Many things are going well. Stephen is adjusting to his new nanny, Liz. He's also rolling well and is astounding me every day with his increasing dexterity. He now eats his solids in his high-chair & has taken to rusks with a passion. The bottle feeding continues to be mainly on his back, but quite happily. Bath time, now taken together, is pure joy. I can't remember when I laughed so much or so heartily.

The remaining problem is sleep, especially at night. Stephen wakes (?) almost two hourly. Usually resettling requires no more than a few mouthfuls of water, restoring the dummy & changing his position. Sometimes he can't seem to resettle at all (especially after 3 a.m.). I then take him into bed with me, which gives us both a little more 'shut-eye'. It certainly isn't deep sleep.

I've tried everything. Even the chiropractor hasn't helped this time. At first I thought it was a head cold, but that's almost gone. Then I thought it was teething, and have used Bonjella. But I see little sign of teeth coming in. Sometimes I give him Panadol of a night but I don't

know if it helps. I've even resorted to a few herbal brews,
Baby's Friend and Soothing Drops.

Food/Sleep Record: Fri 16/7
1. *5.50 a.m. (200 ml.)*
2. *9.15 a.m. (180 ml. + cereal + apple)*
3. *1 p.m. (180 ml. + pumpkin)*
4. *4.45 p.m.(200 ml. + banana)*
5. *6.30 p.m.(herbal 5 ml. + Mylanta + Bonjella). Used
    ritual (bath then cuddle then music). Replaced
    dummy twice. Went off 7 p.m. without rocking.
    Settled on his tummy; hence, didn't tuck him in.
    Resettled/rocked 7.30 p.m.(congested). 8.45 p.m.
    Panadol. 9.10 p.m. Woke. 11.45 p.m. Helped onto
    stomach. 3.15 a.m. Resettled on side. 5.15 a.m.
    Woke up happy. Let him play in bed quietly. Sat
    beside him & patted him off. Slept 7 a.m. to 7.45
    a.m.*

Diary: *Friday 16 July (continued) I'm moving all my files
& books back to the office & will try to settle in* [to work]
*next week. With the little sleep I'm getting, I find the
whole prospect daunting. If retiring were an option, I'd
probably be looking at it. I know I can't afford leave
without pay. Besides my problems now are not
exceptional & other mothers cope. I've decided I'll just do
what has to be done . . . The other thing to think about
is resuming teaching next year (1994). If I design action
learning courses, this should not be too arduous. The*

undergraduate course will focus on the way women's issues are represented and how this affects outcomes. [This eventually became the basis for *Women, Policy and Politics: The Construction of Policy Problems.* Sage, 1999]. *I'd love to offer an Honours course on the politics of motherhood.* [I did offer such a course but there weren't enough takers. Motherhood is not a very sexy subject which, of course, is part of the problem.]

So, despite lack of sleep, I'm feeling remarkably positive. I'm looking forward to doing all sorts of things with Stephen, though I don't know where you fit them in to his feeding/sleeping regime. Note: he feeds every 3 and a half to 4 hours. Feeding, including solids, takes almost an hour. He is supposed to nap one and a half hours in the morning and again in the afternoon. As I see it, this leaves an hour in the morning and one in the afternoon for outings. [This was enforced on us, of course, because I could give Stephen a bottle only at home, in an undisturbed setting].

23 July/93   Some improvements on the sleep scene. Though it takes a while (20 minutes or so) Stephen is falling asleep on his own, at night anyway. Liz (the nanny) and I still rock him off for naps. If we waited for him to do it on his own, the nap time would be over before it began. At night, he still usually stirs and needs resettling after 30-40 minutes. Tonight I'm waiting, so it probably won't happen.

Stephen came through his check-up with flying colours. No need to see the pediatrician again. He's even moved into the above average weight category!

I started attending seminars again this week . . . I think I had some intelligent things to say. I must confess to enjoying the intellectual exercise. I don't suppose I could give it away really, though I also enjoy my time with Stephen. I'm lucky to have both available to me.

Monday 26 July/93   A lovely weekend but another horrendous night & a long morning . . . A few problems with bottles on Saturday. I thought it was the old nightmare recurring but I think he was constipated. It also seems clear that he now wants solids first . . . Today I'll give him solids first for breakfast and let Liz try him with a bottle. Unless she can give him a bottle, my life is very difficult to organise. There are many seminars I can't attend simply because they coincide with a bottle feeding. We'll see how we go this morning.

27 July, Tuesday.   We didn't go well. Stephen wouldn't have a bar of a bottle from Liz . . . He settled on his tummy at first last night & didn't surface till 9.45 p.m. I gave him a little Panadol (I won't tonight!). I heard him crying at 11.45 p.m. but it didn't last long & even briefer crying at 2 a.m. Then soon as he moved at 5.45 a.m. I gave him a bottle & he returned to sleep. Now, why did he sleep through last night? I had the Phenergan [antihistamine with sedative effects] *on hand but didn't use it.*

Wed 28 July   A Typical Day. Is there any such thing? Stephen actually slept through which in itself is atypical. I woke up at 5.30 a.m., wondering if he'd call for a bottle by 6 a.m. or rearrange the schedule yet again. I zipped into the kitchen to change the Milton and begin preparations for the formula—boiling the water. I have a quick cup of coffee to get me started for the day. Stephen calls at 5 minutes before 6. I give him a bottle—never uncomplicated—and put him back to bed. I go to the bathroom to brush teeth, etc. Stephen calls unexpectedly after 30 minutes. He seems to need more sleep so I rock him off. Back to the kitchen to get his breakfast ready & have my own (+ another cup of coffee). He surfaces again & I rock him off again. Back to the kitchen to make the formula, prepare his juice and, yes, again he needs to be rocked off. Finally he surfaces rested and happy at 8.45 a.m. Breakfast is served at 9.15. He rejects the bottle but does well with cereal. Liz arrives and takes over. I head to the office where I clear away some paper work and have morning coffee with Annette. Need to be home for Stephen's lunch bottle. I get there early & put my head down for a nap (e.g. I close my eyes for 15 minutes). Lunch goes well. In the afternoon Yvonne and 9 month old Jacques visit. I walk them home with Stephen in the backpack. He naps. Dinner—a feeding frenzy from 5 p.m. to 5.45 p.m. Annette drops in for a meal of veges. 6.30 p.m. Bath-time. Bedtime ritual. Stephen in bed at 7.15 p.m. Wrestles with sleep for 30 minutes. I have my third glass of wine & wait for him to need resettling, which almost invariably happens. Soon I'll go to bed & the cycle begins again.

Mon. 1 Aug. Had a few tears this morning. Two days in a row Stephen refused breakfast, making it difficult for me to plan the rest of the day. There wouldn't be a problem, of course, if he could feed anywhere and with solids this will soon be the case. We're also moving forward with a training cup so bottle feeds will hopefully soon be a thing of the past.

Thurs. 5 August/93 Last night Stephen couldn't resettle after his traditional half-hour first sleep. That is—boy, is it confusing!—Stephen almost always wakes exactly 30 minutes after going to sleep (naps as well as at night). Usually he is very easy to resettle. Last night there was nothing I could do. I even broke the rules and picked him up, though I didn't rock him off. He just kept crying, so I left him to it for a while. It was agony! Occasionally I'd go in and pat him but he just couldn't resettle. Finally I remembered that one of the 'sleep' books suggested sitting beside him. I did this and held his little hand and in a while he drifted off.

I recall Stephen's odd sleeping pattern, his frequent wakings and need for resettling. I will never know why he always woke up about half-an-hour after going to sleep, both for naps and at night. All I know is that it was exhausting.

Thurs 5 August (continued)   *He woke very bright this morning, unfortunately at 4.30 a.m! I kept trying to tell him he wasn't taking enough milk yesterday to see him through. But Stephen is more and more in control of what he consumes. In fact he sometimes makes me feel quite ridiculous with my attempts to distract him to get him to take more. So, here we are with Stephen 8 months old and a routine yet to be established. It's still unclear how many bottles he'll have today and hence when exactly he'll be hungry. This disturbs me less than it used to. Slowly, oh so slowly, I've come to realise that Robbie Burns must have had parenting in mind when he wrote, 'The best laid plans of mice and men (sic!) gang aft aglay', or something to that effect.*

Sunday 8 August.   *I'm still pretty keen to get him to take that first morning bottle since it's a challenge these days to get him to take the 600 ml. minimum requirements. We've done well today. I've decided to try to find out what he wants when, so I'm offering him small bottles an hour after meals . . . I'm also getting better (at last) at knowing when he's hungry. Finally I no longer have to fear the infant's hunger wail. If anything, now, he just gets grizzly. There remains the problem of just where he will take this bottle. If we don't find some way other than on the rug at home, our activities will be further constrained since I'll have to give him solids and then wait an hour before giving him the bottle.*

Read last night for an hour after Stephen went to bed. First time I was willing to risk it!

Because of the broken nights, I would usually put my head down the moment Stephen did. Even if I knew he would wake me up several times, I felt that I had to snatch every chance for sleep which came available. I can remember trying to hurry myself to sleep. I knew that I had to get to sleep quickly because he would be likely to call out sooner rather than later. I used to count backwards from 1000 to try to get to sleep quickly.

(Tues) 10 August/93   Stephen woke crying at 1.30 a.m. last night. I left him a few minutes feeling that, if he didn't resettle himself, we'd be back in the nightmare where he was waking 4 or 5 times a night. Finally went in to find the poor little lamb had wet himself through. Needless to say, I feel guilty but not as bad as I would have felt had I left him longer.

Thurs. 12 Aug/93   Actually doing a little (paid) work these days. Feels good to be thinking again. My skill for organisation is paying dividends. It's a real challenge to get everything done. Stephen is sleeping better. It's fairly clear the problem was teething. So much for the pediatrician who said that there wasn't a tooth in sight. The feeds (bottle) have lost their trauma as well. I'm using a small bottle which seems to put less pressure on his gums and he's eating so many solids I don't really have to worry about his intake of milk.

The timing remains tricky. Sometimes he doesn't want a bottle until an hour after his (ample) meal & since this can still be done only by me in a quiet room, I have to wait around. This limits the amount of free time to get out & do things with him, since I also have to ensure that he gets a morning and afternoon nap. Speaking of which, he's sleeping soundly now, a little too soundly given that it's almost 4.30 p.m. in the afternoon. I may need to wake him. Geez!!

Chapter 14

Resolution?

With all these changes, you may wonder if there is a purpose to continuing with this recount. Indeed, the end is in sight. In fact, the Feeding/Sleeping Records stop in early September, and the Diary entries peter out after mid-October, 1993, with a few later updates. But an important issue needs to be pursued. I have mentioned several times that the nightmare had quite dramatic effects on my state of mind. I've even retold an incident which I had failed to record where my instability was clear. I became more and more aware that *I* had a problem. You may not be surprised at this. After all, I had had little and broken sleep for nine months. I had faced and managed almost on my own to feed a baby who rejected food. I've tried to explain to people the absolute agony of going to feed an infant who is screaming with hunger only to have him bat the bottle away. I don't think that I can quite communicate that agony. I can only ask you to imagine it. At any rate, the experience took its toll on me, and just maybe on Stephen, though I don't think so. Children are remarkably resilient. I only wish that I had known this earlier. Maybe, just maybe, if I'd known, I wouldn't have suffered so much.

Wed. 18 August/93 Stephen [eight-and-a-half months old] *is doing beautifully. He's eating his solids with gusto. His attitude to bottles remains indifferent. He and Liz [the nanny] are very good together. There's lots of laughter in the house. Very important.*

Tomorrow I see a psychologist to find out if I indeed have a problem over Stephen's eating. I have been a little disturbed at some of my behaviours recently, actually throwing something (not at him) when he refused a bottle. I also still get tense when offering him a bottle. He still takes them lying flat on his back, with me pinning his left arm and keeping his right occupied with toys. Will there be any long-term effects for him of this strange feeding pattern? [Stephen developed an early liking for dangling things from his fingers, from string, from anything. I've always wondered if there is a connection.]

As to my behaviour, there are so many possible causes, I wonder what can be gained from identifying more. I think the key is that I want Stephen to have a schedule, to be predictable. In the past, this has been tied to him having full bottles at least four hourly. Some of this is less of a problem with solids. But I remain tense for the first bottle of the day, because if he doesn't take it, I might have to give him breakfast earlier which will change everything for the day. And the evening bottle always concerns me since I feel that I have a better chance of a good night's sleep if he takes it. This isn't a selfish goal. It's necessary for me to get a good sleep to be able to take care of Stephen properly and to do anything useful at the office (which, after all, pays the bills). So, that's what I think is going on. Let's see if the psychologist agrees.

Friday 27 August/93 Stephen is just about to crawl. Very exciting to see his increasing control of his body. He's had another throat infection over the past week but with the help of antibiotics (again, damn it!), we seem to have defeated it relatively easily.

The psychologist didn't seem to feel that I had a huge problem. She thought that many of my anxieties were quite understandable (bless her!). Hence, she's given me techniques (slow breathing) to control them. In fact, paradoxically, those anxieties have lessened since Stephen's recent illness. I have now seen that he will take from a bottle what he needs and will still go to the next meal. That is, I don't have to worry that he will start screaming from hunger.

Thursday 2 Sept/93 Stephen is nine months old today. Things are going really well & I'm actually feeling fairly much in control. But things happen which still throw me, confuse me. This afternoon he just wouldn't take his nap, screamed on & off for 30 minutes. I lost my cool and shouted. Fortunately, he was making so much noise, he probably didn't hear me.

Sunday 12 Sep/93 We're having a great time. Stephen is wonderful. He's entranced by everything and gives me *great joy. Definitely crawled forward today. Also, rejected a bottle at lunch at a birthday party for a one year old. He was too excited to eat. I was disturbed until I saw that it made no difference to his mood or schedule. No screaming with hunger. Napped for one and a half hours. Only problem now—early waking (5.45 a.m.) and he's still tired. Hence, I have to rock him off or pat him to get him to take a little more sleep.*

Sat night 25th Sept.   I hesitate to write this because I am not pleased with myself & I'm a little worried about what it means. I suppose it would have been more serious had I decided not to write about it.

Eve and her daughter, three year old Vivian, visited today. Everything went well (though they had to go for a walk so Stephen would nap) till dinner. Stephen woke and I knew they would be back shortly so I whacked him into the highchair and tried to get him eating. [I knew that if the visitors returned, they would distract him and he wouldn't eat.] *He was not quite awake and got upset. Then they arrived and, of course, he was too distracted to eat. I got upset/cried. I said he was really hungry but wouldn't eat (Clearly this was inaccurate. Stephen was far from ravenous). I left it a while but kept going back to his dinner. Things were going OK but some over-enthusiastic encouragement from Eve (leaning over Stephen, saying 'ahhhh!') resulted in more tears* [from Stephen]. *Dinner postponed again. Then tried in the walker and was going fine. Since he clearly wasn't eating his usual amount of banana & yogurt, I topped up with Fruche. He choked on this and vomited everything back. I suggested we call it a night.*

I didn't get too upset, bathed Stephen, gave him his bottle and put him to bed. But what has caused me a little concern is the feeling that I will subsequently protect Stephen from future episodes like this one. Am I protecting myself? Must I not come to terms with the fact that Stephen is a complex human being & likes people more than food? Also, skipping the occasional meal won't kill either one of us. I keep saying that my fear is that he won't get through the night and I might not be able to cope. But I've always coped before. I need to think through just what my concern is.

Oct 3—4.15 p.m.   Re the food situation, things are still tricky. Stephen would eat next to nothing at the Edwards' yesterday. Even rejected his favourites, yogurt & banana, and Fruche. I persisted, convinced that he wouldn't sleep through the night without dinner. Managed to trick him, using the dummy, to eat a little. Don't know if I ought to do this. [This trick involved pulling out his dummy and slipping in a spoonful of food before he realised what I was up to.]

4th Oct.   Stephen [now ten months old] *woke only once last night, about 1.30 a.m., quite distressed. I tried settling him & held him. He still screamed, so I gave him .8 ml. of Panadol. I can only assume it's his teeth.*

16th Oct Saturday. Stephen is sleeping well at night. Didn't stir last night. But is rebelling at naps. I think he may be giving the afternoon nap away. This will make it easier to do things in the afternoon + I like him going to bed before 7 p.m.

End of October 1993.   Little time or inclination to make entries. Nearly made one the other day, after my first use of Phenergan. But I realised that I'd done the right thing. Stephen just couldn't settle. I let him cry 30 minutes. Nearly killed me. Now I've learnt something. He can look very, very sleepy & still not be ready for bed. He seems to get a second wind after his bottle. I just have to let him play it out.

So, things are going well. Stephen has dropped his late afternoon nap and, with the aid of daylight saving, we've shifted his lunch to before his big nap—2 hours. He's crawling and beginning to pull himself up. He's gregarious, but entertains himself well. He's perfect! I love him more than life.

Chapter 15

Time Out!

I can remember the day I stopped keeping Feeding/
Sleeping Records. Someone, the nanny I think,
suggested that they were no longer serving any
purpose. Patterns had now emerged, so there was no
point any longer in searching for them. This, I now
realise, is what those records were all about. If I had
it on paper, maybe I could see a pattern, maybe I
could sort things out. My academic training clearly
played a role here.

I don't remember the day I stopped writing the
Diaries. Clearly they too had served a need which
had ceased or been reduced. This could have been a
need to talk to someone, if only to myself, about
what was happening. As the trauma became less,
the entries became fewer. I made a few brief updates
over the next little while on 'landmark' days like
Stephen's first birthday and when he started to walk,
conventional milestones. There is also an entry in
January 1995 which I presume was made one day
when I had rediscovered and reread my accounts,
and wanted to round them off.

These tell only part of the story, however. There were,
you see, lingering effects of the nightmare over the
next few years. I just didn't write about them. I was
too engaged in my paid labour to find the time or
energy to keep records. And the incidents were

isolated and not extraordinary. I continued to need to use slow breathing whenever I fed Stephen and I had to remind myself almost daily not to allow food to become an issue between us. For parents of 'picky' eaters, this will strike a chord. I allowed Stephen to watch television so that I could feed him. I occasionally overfed him, and he vomited. I find it amazing that we have emerged from this period as well, physically and psychologically, as we are.

2 December, 1993 I must make an entry today. Don't know what happened to November. But today is Stephen's first birthday. I sit here—it's 5.30 a.m.— looking at a room full of toys. The little lamb is asleep and should sleep until at least 7 a.m. (yesterday it was 8 a.m!). He also slept through the night. He does this more often now. But I have to wait for him to be ready to go to bed. Last night it was 9.30 p.m, a little late for my liking.

A brief summary of important changes: Stephen is pulling himself up at every opportunity. I'd say another month before his first steps! We went to the clinic on Tuesday and he has been taken off formula. I'm gradually putting him on cow's milk. Soon there will be no more morning mixing, boiling water, sterilising bottles! He said his first word, 'tickle', would you believe? This is due to Liz (the nanny) and her games, e.g. 'round and round the garden, like a teddy bear, etc, etc.' Stephen's favourite past-time until now has been his little trike. Just recently I've been putting him in a small bathing pool (his birthday gift) & he loves it! Problem is, he doesn't want to get out. I'll have to work on this one.

We had a lovely night last night (until 8.30 p.m. at any rate). We played in the pool, sat in the courtyard, had a lovely bath, rolled on the floor, played with Duplo, played our recorders—bashed them on a tray. Earlier in the afternoon (I take over from Liz at 3 p.m.) we did the shopping together. Stephen's beginning to reach out to grab things, but doesn't seem to mind if he fails to make contact . . .

Work proceeds slowly. I have a few commitments looming but, when I've had a good night's sleep, everything seems possible. So, Happy Birthday, little lamb, we've made it!

4 February, 1994   Stephen turned 14 months old two days ago. Yesterday, he started <u>walking</u> from point A to point B, with points getting further and further apart. He's been pushing a trolley with gay abandon for several months. Now, it seems, he's ready to go solo. I'm writing this at 7.30 a.m. waiting for Stephen to <u>wake up</u>. He slept through from 8.30 p.m. last night. Feeding remains a problem area, especially as Stephen now knows what he likes and doesn't like. Liz and I tend to pop things in his mouth. He's often too busy doing other things to *think about food. He still takes a bottle only from me, but we're working on it.*

Stephen continues to have a sunny disposition. His displays of will are few. But, then again, there are very few things he isn't allowed to do!

January, 1995   I want to start a new journal but, until I find the time and energy, I must make a few notes. Stephen and I have just returned from our two-week holiday in Victor Harbor [we moved to Adelaide in the middle of 1994]. *He is now two years old and a bit. Everything is absolutely wonderful. Up until two days ago he called me 'Me'. There is a tape recording of this. Now, I'm 'Mum'. This evening we played on the back lawn and he initiated kissing me and saying 'I love you much'. He also put together a version of 'Happy Birthday to you, Mum!' We are communicating in a fashion I hadn't dreamt possible, even two weeks ago. Today, he graduated from 'Babies' to B-Nursery at childcare. He was keen to shift and wanted to show me everything on my arrival. There is so much that is good—I need a volume!*

17 October, 2001   Looking back, I remain puzzled about the causes of Stephen's feeding disorder. It now seems to me that there wasn't a single cause, or rather that one problem 'fed' another until all the 'causes' got mixed up. I have no doubt that Stephen

was a 'colickly' baby and that I was poorly prepared to deal with this. I also know that the early months of Stephen's life where I attempted breastfeeding and he cried almost non-stop traumatised me. The lack of sleep wore me down. It is also clear that there was an element of post-traumatic rejection after the viral pharangytis. The fact that I was left with the task of getting him to 'feed past the pain' clearly had an impact on me and on my attitude to his feeds. I don't think that I will ever know if he had reflux or not. I do know that he rejected food in many forms and had some distinctly odd eating patterns, for example, crying after a few mouthfuls of solids. I believe that my desperation to get him to feed exacerbated the physiological difficulties. For example, during the period when I deliberately kept the teat lids loose to guarantee a 'decent' feed, there seems little doubt that he gulped air which produced wind.

There are other themes that run through the Diaries and Food Records. The search for a routine is a prominent one. In fact, I now believe that keeping the Food/Sleep Records indicate my desire to try to find a schedule, a pattern I could predict. Some people would say that here the problem was me, that I was an older first-time mother and that I couldn't come to terms with the disruption to my life that comes 'naturally' with an infant. Others would suggest that my personality made this particularly difficult for me. The Diaries note my pride in my ability to organise and my desire to gain 'control'. Some would add that being a professional woman and an academic created particular strains since I tried to understand everything, to make sense of developments which could not be understood rationally. I certainly had difficulty dealing with out-of-control behaviours, such as high-pitched, frantic crying. I am willing to take all these suggestions on board. But I think that it is important to recognise just why I so desperately wanted to find a routine. It seems to me that our story illustrates the routinised nature of modern life and the stresses this creates for mothering and parenting. Again, I find it amazing that in the main we manage to emerge sane from this situation, though there is increasing evidence that many of us are showing signs of strain.

Stephen is now almost nine years old. Last year (2000) I faced a particularly difficult work year. I was holding down a high level administrative post, in addition to a heavy teaching and marking load, publishing commitments and pressure to seek outside funding. I would get up at 4.30 or 5 a.m. at the latest to get some work done before Stephen woke up, in order to create some space later in the day to be a mother (get him from school at a reasonable hour, get homework done, prepare meals, and find time to play). I became ill and had, for the first time in my working life, to take a week off. Stephen became obsessed with schedules. He picked up on my tension and started having difficulty getting to sleep. He became quite agitated if he wasn't in bed 'on time'. This symbiosis between Stephen and me—the ways in which my moods and feelings affect his disposition and habits, and vice versa—is a major theme in our story, another theme that I suspect is relevant in other lives.

This year (2001) I have had study leave and am currently (at the time of writing) on long-service leave. It is ironic in a sense that I should be using these few weeks to revisit the last time I had long-service leave, the time I 'took off' to care for Stephen. It is indeed the first space I have had to undertake this project. I have used this year to show Stephen that life without schedules is both possible and indeed very pleasant. He no longer has trouble getting to sleep. I do wonder, however, if I ought to have shown him this since it is unlikely to match the reality of our lives next year, or of his life in his future.

Food, I am pleased to say, is no longer an issue between Stephen and me, though I can't quite identify when this happened. Through our minor ups and downs, I would repeat as a mantra the message from the psychologist that I not allow food to become an issue between us. As a result, Stephen has an appalling diet. He eats almost no vegetables, hates fruit and loves sweets. I make the same kinds of token gestures to get him to eat 'something healthy' as do other parents who face this situation. But I make a conscious effort not to go 'over the top' about it, to avoid recreating a version of our old nightmare. (Paradoxically, then, food remains an issue!) I console myself that children in other parts of the world manage to survive on much worse diets. In other words I know he will get through this and that he will be 'all right'. I no longer fear that he will starve or that he will scream because he is starving. I didn't have his favourite cereal in stock this morning and in protest he declared that he didn't want *any* breakfast then. There was a time, in the not-too-distant past, when this would have upset me, when I would have insisted that he had 'to eat something'. This morning I replied calmly: 'That is absolutely fine!' I meant it.

This last anecdote suggests that the central problematic in my life with Stephen had never been his rejection of food, though I had thought that to be the case. Rather, the central problematic was *my* fear of food rejection. There are several specific references to this in the text. Now, clearly, a fear of food rejection depends to some extent on food being rejected, and Stephen did more of this than most babies. But many mothers/parents encounter versions of this problem, or of some other, even greater, challenge. In effect then my story offers glimpses into the complexity, the perplexity of mothering. It captures, I hope, some of the dynamic involved in being held solely responsible for a dependent, often very demanding, small human being. If as a society we really want to do something about post-natal depression, it tells us, we must address the isolation, the obsessive claustrophobia[11], associated with this experience.

In the text I suggest that my experience of mothering fits onto a continuum. It reflects specific factors, including coming to motherhood late in life, single parent status, and a difficult infant feeding disorder. Other women's experiences will be different if, for example, they form part of an extended family, if they have more than one child, if a child has a problem more serious than Stephen's. Still, I think that my narrative draws attention to some

---

11   I would like to thank Chris Beasley for this phrase.

commonalities in the experience of mothering which deserve attention.

To different degrees women are left alone to cope with the needs and demands of a tiny vulnerable human being. Often badly sleep deprived, they are expected to produce a happy, healthy and docile child. A host of professionals exists to tell them primarily what they are doing *wrong*, increasing the pressure to perform. Attempts to bring together infant care and paid labour in a society which pretends children do not exist exacerbates this pressure. On every front mothers are expected to behave 'normally', while everything in their experience makes this so very difficult for them to do.

The problem then is not that I came to motherhood with high or unrealistic expectations, only to have them dashed. Rather, the problem is the high expectations placed on mothers—the expectation that they be the same sort of person as they were before motherhood; the simultaneous and contradictory expectation that they now dedicate themselves fully to their child; the expectation that they should endure endless sleepless nights and emerge smiling, competent and content. If they do not do this, there are professionals who will call their confusion and distress 'post-partum depression'.

This only increases the pressure to want to appear 'normal', all the while wondering why they don't feel this way.

My story is unashamedly mother-focused rather than child-focused, because mothers are so often left out of the picture. This is why I believe it so important for women to share their stories of challenge and trauma. Women have been doing this in small groups or on a one-to-one basis for a very long time, in coffee clutches or sitting on a beach or in a few snatched moments queuing at a check-out, telling each other how hard it is and sharing strategies for dealing with a range of challenging situations. But the public face of mothering does not include these stories and I think it should. This is why I have related mine. We need to stop treating the traumas of mothering as dirty little secrets to be whispered when no one is looking. Doubtless these whisperings help ease some tension. But they leave in place the myth of motherhood, the myth that things generally go well and that mothering is easy. In fact, mothering can be lonely and you can often feel depressed. This is not an illness; it is the normal experience of many, many mothers.

It is important to reflect on the kinds of social change which could improve this experience. These are implied rather than directly addressed in this narrative. They would range, in my view, from local, targeted support services to deeper structural transformation. Among the former, alongside 'childcare', there needs to be more attention paid to 'mothercare'. Instead of seeing the goal as the production of the 'best baby', health professionals ought to pay more heed to the difficulties mothers face. Publicly-funded social services could provide home helps in the early days of caring for a new born, community child-minding, and drop-in centres, where the focus is on listening rather than advising. Crucially, such services should be thought of, not as 'compensation' for the trials of mothering, nor as 'protection' for vulnerability, and certainly not as 'special advantages', but as requisite interventions on behalf of a vital social activity, mothering.

At a deeper level, the demands of the 'private' require greater recognition from 'public' institutions. This means more than 'allowing' mothers 'time out' from paid labour. I am thinking here of recent discussions about publicly funded paid maternity leave, and some business commitments to 'family friendly policies'. While these policies are essential, we need a more basic rethinking of the escalating imbalance in our lives between paid work and life at home which leaves so little time for the care of children and of others who need care, including ourselves. This rethinking means recognising that for many people, women and men, the relationships cultivated with loved ones are equally, if not more, important in their lives than paid employment. And yet, as working hours increase—for those of us lucky enough to have jobs—these relationships are being squeezed into smaller and smaller niches. Margaret Thatcher is well known for proclaiming, 'There is no such thing as society'. My fear is that, if we continue in the direction we are going, a direction she strongly endorsed, she may very well prove to be correct. Her comment, I would suggest, was prophesy, not description.

For some time feminists have put on the agenda the need for men to assume greater responsibility for domestic labour and childrearing duties. The Swedes have led the way with this agenda, and have recognised that, in order for this to occur, employers must rethink the current image of the ideal employee as workaholic. This is not likely to be a popular suggestion in times like these. However, it is only when care for dependents is elevated to recognition as a valuable social undertaking that it will cease being the lonely task of isolated individuals, mainly women. One step towards this recognition, I believe, is exposing the underside of real-life mothering.

Chinese Medicine for Women
Bronwyn Whitlocke

Bronwyn Whitlocke presents a comprehensive
guide for women to understanding their bodies in
terms of the holistic approach of traditional
Chinese medicine. A good basic guide for women
seeking an alternative to western treatments.

Heather Nix, *The Republican*

ISBN: 1-875559-70-1

Shiatsu Therapy for Pregnancy
Bronwyn Whitlocke

Shiatsu Therapy for Pregnancy is an instructive
manual for pregnant women, practitioners,
partners, and birthing partners caring for pregnant
women.

ISBN: 1-875559-81-7

Vaccination Against Pregnancy:
Miracle or Menace?
Judith Richter

Richter's serious and compelling critique of
immunological contraceptives is a major
contribution to the international women's health
movement.

Betsy Hartmann

ISBN 1-875559-57-4
Available from Spinifex only in Australia and New
Zealand

A Passion for Friends:
Toward a Philosophy of Female Affection
Janice Raymond

This feminist classic explores the many
manifestations of friendship between women, and
examines the ways women have created their own
communities and destinies through friendship. A
tough and clear-sighted analysis to read again and
again.

ISBN: 1-876756-08-X

**Women as Wombs: Reproductive Technology
and the Battle Over Women's Freedom**
Janice Raymond

A strongly written, carefully reasoned critique of
the reproductive liberalism that . . . lies behind
current concepts of reproductive choice.

K. Kaufmann

ISBN: 1-875559-41-8 (pb) ISBN: 1-875559-26-4 (hb)

**Living Laboratories:
Women and Reproductive Technologies**
Robyn Rowland

Convincing and terrifying.

Fay Weldon

A strong and powerful book, with the pace of a
detective story, that challenges assumptions,
sharpens awareness, and explores a feminist
morality towards reproductive technology.

Sheila Kitzinger

ISBN: 0-725106-99-9
(Available from Spinifex in Australia and New
Zealand only)

Patient No More: The Politics of Breast Cancer
Sharon Batt

The international best-selling book on breast
cancer.
> Peter Thomson, ABC Radio National

ISBN: 1-875559-39~6
(Available from Spinifex in Australia and New
Zealand only)

**The Menopause Industry: A Guide to Medicine's
"Discovery" of the Mid-Life Woman**
Sandra Coney

An antidote to the flood of information extolling
HRT . . . a must read for women of all ages.
> Jill Farrar, *New Woman*

ISBN: 1-875559-14-0
(Available from Spinifex in Australia and New
Zealand only)

Get Used To It:
Children of Gay and Lesbian Parents
Myra Hauschild and Pat Rosier

Essential reading for young people, teachers and anyone working with youth.

ISBN: 1-875559-91-4

Glory
Sarah Brill

An impressive new voice in youth literature. Sarah Brill writes with sensitivity of one girl's struggle with herself, her life and her family.

ISBN: 1-876756-25-X

HELP! I'm Living with a ~~Man~~ Boy
Betty McLellan

With a mixture of sensitivity and humour McLellan puts forward some thoughtful strategies to help men understand the difference between mumbled promises of future help and solid action.

The Sunday Times

ISBN 1-875559-79-5

Beyond Psychoppression
Betty McLellan

What is the basis of self help? Is it useful? How do therapeutic programs based on twelve-step programs, self-help and new age philosophy contribute to the political and social freedom of women? The personal is political, but is the individual political? These questions are thoroughly explored by one of Australia's most highly respected feminist therapists.

ISBN 1-875559-33-7

The Anger of Aubergines
Bulbul Sharma

Food as a passion, a gift, a means of revenge, even a source of power.

ISBN: 1-876756-01-2
(Available from Spinifex in Australia, New Zealand and the UK)

She's Fantastical
Lucy Sussex and Judith Raphael Buckrich (Eds)
Shortlisted for the 1995 World Fantasy Award

Fantasy has always been a rebel's mode, a means of sneakily saying unwelcome or disturbing things about one's society, or of offering a more or less plausible alternative to it. The stories and poems in this book are all, in one way or another, fantastic, all are rebellious, subversive, critical, or teasing, cheerfully or fiercely knocking the posts from under the Status Quo.

Ursula K. Le Guin

ISBN 0-908205-12-0

If you would like to know more about Spinifex Press
write for a free catalogue or visit our website

SPINIFEX PRESS
PO Box 212 North Melbourne
Victoria 3051 Australia
<http://www.spinifexpress.com.au>